CUE CARDS *for* LIFE

"A very helpful book and a very easy read."

— Susan Forward, PhD
New York Times best-selling author of
Toxic Parents and *Emotional Blackmail*

"*Cue Cards for Life* is a great recipe for how to make the best of all your relationships and manage the issues that we all face. The strategies in the book are practical and easy to use—you'll enjoy reading them all!"

— Dr. Terri Orbuch
Relationship expert, therapist, and author of
5 Simple Steps to Take Your Relationship from Good to Great

"This book gives great practical advice with a 'nuts-and-bolts' approach to the relationships we all have in our lives. The Cue Cards give you the the 'basic gems' or guidelines that we should be mindful of when we are interacting with others we care about. The author then provides examples for the reader, or the 'how to's and whys of communication.'"

— Kristy Shadt, MFT, RPT-S, SEP

"This is a great book for everyone who wants to improve their relationships and who hasn't got a relationship that could be improved. The simplicity and straightforward approach of *Cue Cards for Life* is compelling and powerful. I am looking forward to recommending this book to my clients and to my classes in family relationships. When all is said and done, the most important thing in a person's life is their relationships. This book empowers people to get the most from those relationships. Congratulations, Ms. Steinorth, your book is spectacular and fun. What a rare find!"

—Lee Reid, PhD, MFT

"As a licensed therapist with a practice consisting primarily of teenagers and their families, I found the 'Cue Cards for Parents with Teens' section particularly useful. Steinorth has managed to highlight the most significant dimensions of a healthy parent–teen relationship and has provided a framework for communication that parents can easily build upon. For those families unable to spend a large amount of time and money in therapy, *Cue Cards for Life* can be a wonderful resource for healing and health in their family."

—Monique Muther, MA, MFT
San Diego, CA

CUE CARDS for LIFE

THOUGHTFUL TIPS
FOR BETTER RELATIONSHIPS

★ CHRISTINA STEINORTH, MA, MFT ★

Hunter House PUBLISHERS

Ordering

Trade bookstores in the U.S. and Canada please contact
Publishers Group West
1700 Fourth Street, Berkeley CA 94710
Phone: (800) 788-3123   Fax: (800) 351-5073

For bulk orders please contact
Special Sales
Hunter House Inc., PO Box 2914, Alameda CA 94501-0914
Phone: (510) 899-5041   Fax: (510) 865-4295
E-mail: sales@hunterhouse.com

Individuals can order our books by calling **(800) 266-5592**
or from our website at **www.hunterhouse.com**

Project Credits

Cover Design: Brian Dittmar Design, Inc.
Book Production: John McKercher
Developmental Editor: Jude Berman
Copy Editor: Kelley Blewster
Indexer: Candace Hyatt
Managing Editor: Alexandra Mummery
Acquisitions Assistant: Susan Lyn McCombs
Editorial Intern: Tu-Anh Dang-Tran
Special Sales Manager: Judy Hardin
Publicity Assistant: Martha Scarpati
Rights Coordinator: Candace Groskreutz
Customer Service Manager: Christina Sverdrup
Order Fulfillment: Washul Lakdhon
Administrator: Theresa Nelson
Computer Support: Peter Eichelberger
Publisher: Kiran S. Rana

For Matthew
Thank you for your inspiration and support,
which has known no boundaries.
I love you, my dear, sweet husband.

For my mother
Thank you for always encouraging my strengths.
I am blessed to have you in my life.

Hunter House Inc., Publishers
PO Box 2914
Alameda CA 94501-0914

Library of Congress Cataloging-in-Publication Data
Steinorth, Christina.
Cue cards for life : thoughtful tips for better relationships /
Christina Steinorth.
p. cm.
Includes bibliographical references and index.
ISBN 978-0-89793-616-3 (pbk.)
ISBN 978-0-89793-627-9 (ebook)
1. Interpersonal relations.   2. Interpersonal communication.
I. Title.
HM1106.S757 2012
302—dc23   2012019226

Printed and bound by Sheridan Books, Ann Arbor, Michigan
Manufactured in the United States of America

9 8 7 6 5 4 3 2 1   First Edition   13 14 15 16 17

Contents

☆   ☆   ☆

Important Note

The material in this book is intended to provide ideas and suggestions for improving social interactions and relationships.

The author and publisher assume no responsibility for any outcome of using the suggestions in this book. We hope everyone will use them with common sense and in the positive spirit in which they are intended. If you have questions concerning your social interactions or family or other relationships, consult a qualified counselor or mental-health professional.

Introduction

*E*very day when I'm out and about on my regular business, I observe casual interactions between people that are potentially harmful to their relationships, and I ask myself, "Why are they doing that?!" Because I'm a psychotherapist, I'm sure that I'm more sensitive to these exchanges than other folks are. I really don't go looking for them, but I can't help noticing.

At the market the other day I was standing in the checkout line and I overheard a conversation taking place behind me. I'm pretty sure it was between a son and his mother. The son was telling his mom how he'd just been elected class president. It was obvious to me from his tone that he was excited and proud of his accomplishment. He also talked about how surprised he was that he'd been elected. While it's quite possible she was just having a bad day and maybe was running a bit late, what really struck me was how uninterested his mother seemed. She was flipping through a magazine, not making eye contact with him (I admit I peeked at them), and when she did respond, she said, "Shouldn't you start looking into transferring colleges? If you don't do it this year, it'll be too late." Not once did the mother show a bit of excitement or happiness about her son's accomplishment.

Of course, in my therapist's mind I was thinking, "In ten years when he's married and has a family of his own, his mother is going to wonder, 'Why doesn't my son ever call me?'" Well, lady, it's because when your son *did* try to communicate and connect with you, you didn't seem the least bit interested, and when he was sharing an accomplishment he was obviously proud of, you didn't even acknowledge it—*that's* why your son won't be calling you.

That's kind of a lot to extrapolate from a conversation in the grocery store checkout line, you're probably thinking. Yes, it is, but here is my point: It's these little everyday interactions that, over time, add up and cause the biggest problems in relationships.

In another example, years ago my husband and I were friends with a couple who frequently invited us to their family events, which were usually well attended by friends and family alike. At these events, I remember the grandmother of the family often commenting on women who had blonde hair: "Isn't she a pretty blonde?" Or, "Look at what beautiful blonde hair she has." Well, the couple eventually had a beautiful daughter. She was smart, had good social skills, was well behaved—just a really good kid. One year we were invited to her birthday party and she received as a gift a doll with blonde hair. Her father took the doll from her right after she opened it and said, "Don't worry, we'll return it." Noticing that I was watching the exchange with a puzzled look, he told me, "We only get her dolls with dark hair, because for some reason she thinks only blonde girls are pretty, so we are trying to teach her that brunettes are beautiful, too."

Obviously, I wasn't the only one who had paid attention to the grandmother's comments about girls with "pretty blonde hair."

Now, I'm 100 percent sure the grandmother of this young girl never intended to make her beautiful brunette grand-daughter feel unattractive. In fact, she would probably feel terrible if she knew that her words made her granddaughter believe she wasn't pretty. Still, I found it interesting how even at a young age seemingly insignificant comments can have such an impact. And this is what I'm talking about: The little things people say and do every day that they never give much thought to can actually matter a great deal.

When I witness exchanges like these, I often think, "Wow, if he would have just done this, how much more constructive it would have been," or, "If she had just said that, how much happier everyone would be." (And how they would probably not end up sitting on my therapy couch a few years down the line.)

In the checkout line, if the mother had told her son, "Wow, that's fantastic! Congratulations! I'm proud of you!" the son would probably have felt more validated, which would encourage him to continue sharing things with his mother for the rest of his life. If the grandmother of the young girl had perhaps been less vocal in her admiration of other women's "pretty blonde hair," maybe her granddaughter would realize that "pretty" comes in all colors.

Little things.

Simple things.

Little, simple things that over time make big differences in relationships.

✰✰ Why I Wrote This Book ✰✰

In my work with clients over the years, I've noticed that one of the ways I've been most able to help people has been in improving their everyday interactions with others. I've learned that most of my clients actually *have* the skills they need to fix their relationships, but when they get caught up in their day-to-day lives they kind of go on autopilot and stop really paying attention and using those skills.

If the mother in the grocery store had put a moment's thought into how she could better respond to her son, she would have realized he was excited and proud about his election achievement and I'm sure she would have used the opportunity to share his excitement and connect with him. Likewise, the grandmother probably knew that kids, including her granddaughter, are very impressionable. I'm sure if the grandmother overheard someone telling her granddaughter, "Oh, you'd be so much prettier if you were blonde," she would step in and ask the person not to talk to her granddaughter like that, and would reassure her granddaughter that she was beautiful as she was.

See what I'm getting at? The grandmother just didn't put a lot of thought into what she said and how it might be interpreted by others—even her six-year-old granddaughter.

My point is—people do this all the time.

In fact, we often put more thought into what we're going to have for dinner than into what we say to others, and, perhaps more importantly, we often fail to consider how others will interpret or be affected by our thoughtless words and actions.

At some point I realized that what brought people to my therapy couch was years and years of little things like these adding up to big things, which eventually made them feel their relationships were no longer working—and they didn't know how to fix them. When they finally came to see me, were these people looking for long-winded explanations about why their relationships had broken down? No. Were they looking for lots of reflective listening? No. What they were really hoping for was short, actionable guidance they could put to use immediately—ideas or advice that would help them get their relationships back on track.

It was certainly no coincidence that when I was able to break down the information my clients needed into short, action-oriented suggestions they could easily remember and apply, they got more from therapy.

So that's what I began to do in most therapy sessions. I created tips that could be easily remembered, could be easily applied, and, perhaps most importantly, could bring almost immediate improvement to my clients' relationships. I referred to them as cues, and I created Cue Cards that clients could physically or figuratively carry around with them in their back pocket (so to speak) for use when they needed them.

It worked like a charm.

✩✩ How to Use This Book ✩✩

Over the years I kept track of the most common relationship problems people seem to encounter, and in this book I've compiled the Cue Cards that seemed to be the most helpful in dealing with these issues. The book is designed so you don't have to read it from cover to cover. The Cue Cards are arranged in well-defined, situation-specific chapters, and I encourage you to use the book as you would an encyclopedia. Everyone should read the first chapter—it provides a solid foundation for all of your relationship interactions. After that, just turn to the chapter that applies to your situation and use what you need.

If you are having difficulties in your love relationships, take a look at Chapter 2 to help get things back on track. If you are planning a family event such as a wedding—whether you are the bride-to-be, the groom, or the parents—check out Chapter 3, "Marriages, Babies, In-Laws, and All Things Family" to give you a leg up on how to reduce the possibility of conflict during the get-togethers and celebrations that usually take place during major life transitions. If unruly teens are your problem, see Chapter 4.

If you are a woman and you see something you would like the man in your life to read, don't tell him to read the whole book—just pick the Cue Cards you want him to look at and leave it at that. I promise you, you will have a much easier time getting him to read a few Cue Cards than an entire book. And who knows? Once he reads the pages you've selected, he may find them so helpful he will read the whole book.

Try this approach and you will see how simple it is. Using these Cue Cards, my clients have been able to reduce their conflicts and misunderstandings and improve their relationships. With this book you will be able to do the same.

The advice in this book will immediately help to make your relationship problems more manageable. Hopefully it will help you get them under control *before* they reach a crisis point. If you have a relationship issue that has reached a crisis point already, they will help you calm things down a bit so you have time to think more logically and then wisely take the action that is needed.

Even though life can be complicated, there really isn't any reason for your relationships to be. My simple, straightforward, easy-to-use Cue Cards, when used consistently, will make lasting, positive changes in the majority of your relationships. As a bonus, they'll eventually aid other areas of your life because you will be able to utilize the skills you learn in new situations. Help doesn't need to be complicated to be meaningful. If you're like me, you just need some thoughtful guidanceMy hope is that *Cue Cards for Life* will point you in the right direction.

I wish you and your loved ones much happiness and joy in your relationships.

The Basics

*T*he key to improving all of your relationships is to build a basic set of relationship skills. That's what the Cue Cards in this chapter cover. Once you have them down, they will provide a great foundation for all of your interactions.

Though you may at first feel a little awkward incorporating the basic Cue Cards into your daily exchanges with others, I assure you, when you use them consistently, in time they will become second nature. As with any new skill—whether related to a sport, playing a musical instrument, or your job—the more you work on utilizing it, the easier it will become. Granted, some people will pick up these skills faster than others, but I urge you to avoid becoming frustrated and giving up. Instead of striving for perfection, aim for improvement. As they say, Rome wasn't built in a day.

If you work on getting this basic set of Cue Cards down, the more situation-specific Cue Cards in the following chapters will come to you more easily, and you will eventually be able to execute them with fluidity.

✩✩ Being a Good Listener ✩✩

There is much more to being a good listener than nodding your head when someone speaks and offering the occasional affirmation. Really listening is an art comprised of many elements, and when done well it helps you connect better with others. The Cue Cards listed here will help you listen more effectively and start you down the road to improving almost every relationship in your life.

> **CUE CARDS**
> To be a good conversationalist, you must be a good listener.

You will be more effective in your communication with others if you learn how to truly listen, stay engaged in conversations, and let the other person know through your words and your actions that what they have to say is important to you.

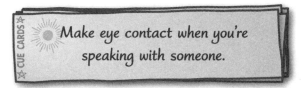

CUE CARDS

Make eye contact when you're speaking with someone.

In Western cultures, making eye contact with the person you are speaking with is seen as polite. When you make and maintain eye contact with a person, you indicate to them that you are interested in what they have to say. Have you ever tried talking with someone who is watching television or looking at some type of electronic device rather than at you? If so, it wouldn't surprise me if you felt that person was distracted. While it's possible they heard every word you said—after all, some people are great at multitasking—it's more likely that you felt they weren't very interested in what you had to say. Making eye contact helps you establish a rapport with the person who is speaking to you. Keep in mind, however, that it's important to be culturally sensitive as well; in some countries, *not* making eye contact actually shows respect.

When you make eye contact with someone, be careful not to cross the line into staring, which tends to make others uncomfortable. If you have fallen out of the habit of making eye contact, try practicing it in a mirror while you maintain a pleasant facial expression. Continued practice with this exercise will help you improve this skill.

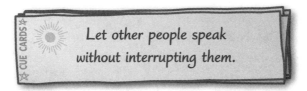

Good listeners listen to what other people say without interrupting them. I'm sure everyone reading this knows someone who is guilty of interrupting. Perhaps you are guilty of it sometimes yourself. Not only is it rude to interrupt, but it often causes people to lose track of their thoughts and derails the flow of conversation. If you accidentally interrupt someone, apologize, bring the topic back to where it was prior to the interruption, and let the speaker finish what he or she has to say.

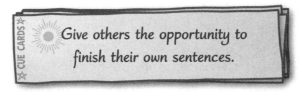

There will be times when you feel you are so "in sync" with another person that you will be inclined to finish their sentences. There also may be times when it seems someone is struggling to make their point, and you may think you know pretty well where he or she is going with the conversation and so you feel inclined to finish the sentence for them as a way of "helping." It is usually best not to act on this impulse. Finishing another person's sentences is just another form of interruption. If you have ever dealt with someone who does this, you've probably experienced some level of frustration, even if it's minor. At a minimum, this habit can be a nuisance; in its extreme, it is irritating and rude. If you find yourself finishing other people's sentences, ask someone close to you to remind you when you do it. Awareness is the key to overcoming bad habits.

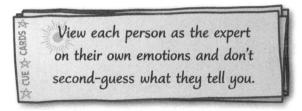

CUE CARDS

View each person as the expert on their own emotions and don't second-guess what they tell you.

Have you ever told someone how you felt about something only to have them say, "Oh, you don't really mean that"?

Unfortunately, it's a very common response. Most of us automatically tend to respond to other people's thoughts and feelings from *our own* viewpoint. What I've learned in working with clients over the years is that if someone tells you they feel or believe something, *they mean it.* If you want to take your relationship skills from good to great, one of the best things you can do is to actually listen to another person and believe that they mean and feel what they have just said they mean and feel.

Taking another person's point of view into account is essential for effective communication. If no one really means what they say, how could anything said by anyone possibly be trusted? When someone tells you they are hurting, take it at face value that they are hurting. Do not substitute your own feelings or judgment for what you are being told, or decide they are "overreacting." To understand this concept more clearly, try to see the person speaking as an expert. Because, in fact, they *are* an expert on their own feelings. Most of us would be reluctant to question an expert's opinion, right? Let's say you take your dog to the vet and are told she has kennel cough. It is unlikely you will disagree with the vet and say, "I think you're wrong. I think she just has something stuck in her throat." Obviously, you are paying your veterinarian for his diagnostic skills. Why would you second-guess him? The same is true in conversation with others. When someone tells you something about their feelings, try not to second-guess their meaning or intent. When you think of the other person as an expert on their own emotions, you are less likely to be perceived as being insensitive and out of touch.

☆☆ Respecting Feelings ☆☆

You can draw people closer to you by demonstrating that you are aware and respectful of their feelings. The Cue Cards below will help you develop this skill.

> ☆ CUE CARDS ☆
>
> *Nonverbal communication can be just as important as what is said.*

Our communication with others is filled with lots of nonverbal information. Our tone, rhythm, and the volume at which we speak, as well as our body language, can sometimes reveal as much as if not more than what we say. They can indicate if we are sincere, curious, judgmental, or even bored. When you pay attention to another person's nonverbal communication it will help you understand that person better. For example, has your spouse or significant other ever looked troubled or low, only to answer "I'm fine" when asked if anything is wrong? In this situation, it may help to improve your communication with one another if you point out to your partner that their nonverbal cues (i.e., appearance, tone, body language) don't seem to match what they are saying: "Well, you say you're fine, but you look worried. Are you sure everything is okay?" If the answer is still "I'm fine," then he or she is either fine (remember the preceding Cue Card), or isn't ready to talk about what is going on.

Of course, you probably would not want to approach someone you don't know very well about a significant disconnect between their words and their nonverbal communication, but if you share a close, personal relationship with someone, checking out a discrepancy like the one described above may help them feel more at ease with you and in turn feel more open to sharing their true feelings.

Keep in mind that it's usually best to ask about your partner's true feelings in a polite, nonaccusatory manner. If you put others on the defensive, they will be unlikely to share their true feelings. If you said, "You always say you're fine, but you look angry. I don't believe you," you have essentially called your spouse a liar. In that case, it is doubtful your spouse will tell you what is truly going on because you have approached them with hostility. When someone you are speaking with is not being totally honest with you, gently inquiring about the inconsistency sends the message that you have a genuine concern for their emotional well-being and are attuned to their feelings. Paying attention to nonverbal communication will make you a better listener and in turn may make others feel more comfortable talking with you.

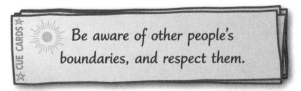

CUE CARDS

Be aware of other people's boundaries, and respect them.

We all learn, sooner or later, that people are different. You yourself have things you are comfortable discussing with others and things you are not. The things you are comfortable discussing may not be the same for your spouse, best friend, coworker, or the person sitting next to you on the bus. And most of us have some subjects we simply do not discuss with anyone—even our most trusted friends and family members. Just as you have things that are very personal to you, remember that others do, too. Where we draw the line about things we are willing to discuss and share with others is a *boundary*, and for effective and meaningful communication, boundaries need to be respected, whether you agree with them or not.

There is no "one size fits all" approach to determining appropriate boundaries. They differ from person to person and are often directly influenced by social and cultural norms. If the person you're speaking with seems uncomfortable discussing a topic you have brought up, do not try to make light of it or cajole her or him into talking about it. Try to pick up on the social or behavioral cues the person is sending out and act on their signals to change the subject. When you respect another's boundaries, you send the message that you respect the person. When you try to push through someone's boundaries—even if it is with good intentions and in a joking way—at the very least you make the other person uncomfortable. At the worst, you give them the impression that their feelings are unimportant to you. In addition, you send the message that you are putting your needs—in this case the need to know what it is that makes them uncomfortable—before theirs.

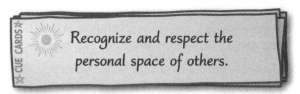

Recognize and respect the personal space of others.

While you are paying attention to nonverbal communication, it is also important to respect others' personal space. Many people greet and part from each other with some type of physical gesture, be it a hug, kiss, or handshake. Some people stand very close to others when they speak (in some cultures, it is normal for *everyone* to stand close to one another when speaking). Each individual has a personal space, an area they want to maintain around their body to be comfortable when having a conversation. There is no right or wrong distance, and the person you are conversing with will most likely stand as close to you as they feel comfortable doing. Strive to be sensitive to others' personal space during greetings and partings, as well as during conversations.

I'm sure through your own experiences you are aware that some people are more touchy-feely than others, so it's useful to recognize how much touch a person feels comfortable with. It is completely possible to have a great conversation with someone and then end with an extremely awkward moment when you bear-hug him or her and they stiffen up like a board. When in doubt, keep your hands and body to yourself.

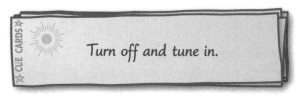

CUE CARDS
Turn off and tune in.

Many would think it an obvious consideration to put a personal communication device away when interacting with others face to face, but unfortunately it is not. Just about anywhere we go we see signs—in doctor's offices, libraries, and spas—reminding us to curb our phone use. We even have laws making it illegal to text while driving. Wherever we turn, we are reminded to silence our phones. This is good advice on many levels. It seems that as a society we have yet to learn how to integrate our personal communication devices into our face-to-face interactions. Don't get me wrong; I think it's great that we have the ability to stay in touch at a moment's notice, but personal communication devices can also cause a great deal of harm to our relationships.

One time I was out with my husband at a restaurant, and I watched a couple at another table spend the evening in silence as they animatedly texted away on their smart phones. When it came time to leave, the man, in an ever-so-gentlemanly fashion, helped his date from her chair and they walked out arm-in-arm. Not once, other than when ordering their meals, did the two of them speak with one another. In another example, the mother of a fifteen-year-old girl told me how she drove her daughter and a friend to the movies, and during the entire car ride both young women sat in silence as they texted away on their respective devices. The two friends never interacted even though they were sitting next to each other in the backseat of a car.

More and more often, I see couples who are doing things together but not engaged in conversation with one another because they are texting someone else or are on their cell phones talking to others. With all of life's demands, it is crucial to make time every day to engage in uninterrupted communication with your loved ones. Personal electronic devices are fantastic when, as with other things in life, they are used in moderation. If you are having a good conversation with your spouse and your cell phone rings, refrain from answering it; whoever is calling can leave a message.

Studies repeatedly show the importance of connecting with your partner to maintain a healthy relationship. Strive to have at least one hour a day of uninterrupted one-on-one time with your spouse or partner. If that isn't possible, aim for more frequent ten-to-fifteen minute connections with your spouse or partner. It does not take much effort to accomplish that. Have light conversation, go for a walk together, or spend a few minutes recapping your day before bed. However you do it, take time to touch base, and do your best to ensure that time is uninterrupted. If you get a call or receive a text, let it wait. Make your partner and your children your number-one priority.

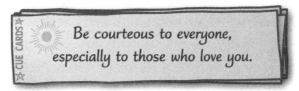

Be courteous to everyone, especially to those who love you.

Although, as a therapist, I see it again and again, it never ceases to amaze me how some people treat strangers and acquaintances with more kindness and gentleness than they treat those closest to them. It's as though their loved ones are supposed to tolerate rude, inconsiderate, or sometimes cruel behavior. I think it can be very easy to start taking your partner (or other loved ones) for granted. From what I've observed, this is where many relationships run into difficulty. Spouses forget how to court one another, and after a time they wonder why their partner seems to lose interest in them. When I refer to courting behavior, I am not talking about flowers, wine, and chocolate. I am talking about everyday considerateness and thoughtful acts. Tell your partner when they look good, kiss each other before you separate for the day, hug frequently. Showing affection does not take a lot of effort; it takes *consistent* effort.

The same thing goes for close relationships with other loved ones: children, parents, and close friends. Remember, every action you take in any relationship either builds the relationship or damages it, so I urge you to take time to think about what you say to and how you interact with the ones you care for. Take even more time to think about the impact your words and actions will have on the relationship. We are generally attracted to and interested in people who make us feel better about ourselves. Just think—would you rather be around someone who never seems to have a nice word to say about you, or would your rather be around someone who lifts your spirits? Just because you are close to someone doesn't mean you should stop being considerate of their feelings.

☆☆ Cue Cards for Social Sensitivity ☆☆

The ability to keep conversations flowing and to address uncomfortable situations is an art. Let the Cue Cards below help you build these skills.

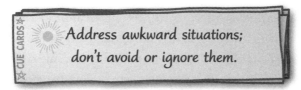

CUE CARDS

Address awkward situations; don't avoid or ignore them.

No one likes an awkward situation, regardless of what it is. It could be something as simple as letting someone know she has spinach in her teeth, or as sensitive as dealing with a friend's husband who seems to get very drunk at every party. When awkward things happen, most people try to look the other way and carry on as if nothing is wrong. I'm quite sure you've noticed that, most of the time, this doesn't work. Ignoring an uncomfortable social situation usually only increases people's discomfort. More to the point, ignoring it does not make it go away.

When awkward social situations arise, it is often quite helpful to break the tension by addressing the incident that everyone knows about but no one wants to mention. The key is to do so thoughtfully and, if possible, in private. Sometimes just calling attention to the awkward situation will reduce the tension immediately. Let's say you are sitting next to a coworker who is about to make a presentation, and you notice her top has slipped down and her bra is showing. Believe me when I tell you that your coworker would be much happier if you quietly and delicately mention that she needs to adjust her top, rather than feeling embarrassed later when she discovers that she just spoke to fifty people with her bra showing.

Or let's say you're dealing with a more serious issue, such as the spouse of a friend who drinks too much at social gatherings. Your friend is probably well aware of the fact her husband drinks too much, but she may feel too embarrassed to talk about it with anyone. If you call her privately and say, "I've noticed your husband is drinking a little more than he probably should. Is there anything I can do to help?" your friend may actually be relieved that she has someone she can confide in about the issue. I urge you to use caution, though; in situations involving more serious alcohol or drug use, regardless of how gently you address it, some people may become angry with you. In that case, it's okay to reassure the person that you aren't trying to intrude on their personal life. Tell her that you are there for her if she ever needs to talk, and drop the matter. While she may remain angry with you and never take you up on your offer to talk about it, you have addressed an issue that may be causing a problem in your relationship. Now that it is out in the open, you can decide how you would like to proceed with your friendship, and she will most likely understand.

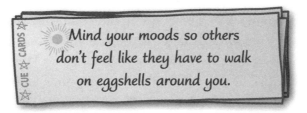

CUE CARDS ☆ ☆ ☆

Mind your moods so others
don't feel like they have to walk
on eggshells around you.

Everyone has moods. Good, bad, or indifferent, moods are a fact of life. What differentiates adults from children is the ability to exercise impulse control and articulate how we feel. Two-year-olds have tantrums because they do not possess the verbal skills to express their frustrations and pain. Teens are also notoriously moody for a variety of reasons we will discuss in Chapter 4. As we mature, though, we develop the vocabulary needed to express how we are feeling, and our brain develops the capacity to place a filter between what we think and what we say. Generally speaking, anyone over the age of twenty-one who is in good physical and mental health should be able to express how they feel in a socially appropriate manner and should be able to refrain from emotional outbursts under most circumstances.

We are all probably guilty of flying off the handle in times of high stress, but when inconsistencies in mood become the norm rather than the exception, it's time to figure out what is causing your mood swings. Generally, people closest to you will offer support when you need it, but I guarantee they will soon start to put some distance between themselves and you if you turn them into an emotional punching bag. When your moods are predictably unpredictable, you run a high risk of making others feel like they must "walk on eggshells" around you. This is never a good thing for any relationship, be it with your spouse, your children, or your coworkers. Some temperamental people claim, "That's just the way I am." Well, that may be true, but if you want people to view you as an adult, you will need to get that behavior under control. If most twenty-one-year-olds can do it, so can you. Even-temperedness is attractive. Volatility is not.

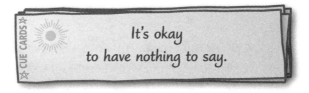

It's okay
to have nothing to say.

A pause in conversation is quite normal, and sometimes so is not knowing what to say. If you find yourself in this situation, relax. It's okay to have periods of silence when you interact with others. In fact, sometimes it's better to have nothing to say than to fill a gap in the conversation with empty words.

> ☆ CUE CARDS ☆
>
> **In all aspects of communication, timing is everything.**

Try to be aware of what is going on with a person when you're talking with him or her. Does your spouse seem busy or stressed with work? If so, it is probably not a good time to have a talk about your relationship or another serious topic. Sure, there will be instances when something needs to be discussed immediately (e.g., an accident), but more often than not this will not be the case. It is unrealistic to expect another person to be emotionally available to you twenty-four hours a day, seven days a week. Be sensitive to what is going on with the person you want to talk to; do your best to ensure that they are in the right frame of mind to receive the message you want to send. When you are mindful of timing and sensitive to the other person's frame of mind, you stand a much better chance of having the conversation go the way you intend.

Cue Cards for Love Relationships

*A*s anyone who has been in a long-term partnership knows, sometimes relationships take just as much work during the good times as they do during the bad. Our love relationships can add a great deal of pleasure and richness to our lives. Science even shows that people are happier and healthier when they are in a good relationship. But what keeps them that way? Is it having things in common? Good communication? Great sex?

It's all those things and more.

With all of the distractions in today's world, it is very easy to lose sight of our connection to our partner. Many of us in long-term relationships start to assume we know what is important to our mates, and we can fall into a pattern of thinking that what is important to *us* is equally important to them. In many cases, this simply isn't true—and we should never assume that it is. Once we make these types of assumptions, what usually happens is that our partners begin to feel disconnected from us.

My work with couples over the years has shown me that there are many pieces to the healthy-relationship puzzle. I have found that the happiest couples, both inside and outside the therapy room, not only demonstrate an awareness of what is important to their partners; they also seem to possess a set of basic skills and understandings that many folks have difficulty remembering day-to-day. The Cue Cards in this chapter will remind you of those skills and will help improve your love relationship almost immediately.

This chapter is divided into three sections. The first section consists of general, or perhaps we should call them universal, Cue Cards, behaviors that must be present in every relationship to keep it healthy. Next is a section about how to handle disagreements and arguments. The last section comprises Cue Cards that will help you nurture your relationship and maintain and grow your feelings of love for one another. These are pointers that your partner may never even know you are using, but they will have a *direct* impact on improving your relationship.

✰✰ General Cues for a Healthy Relationship ✰✰

Let's look at Cue Cards that will help you get your love relationship on the right track and keep it there.

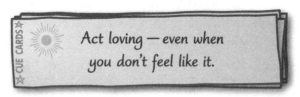

CUE CARDS

Act loving — even when
you don't feel like it.

As much as possible, and even when you're not feeling like it, act loving toward your partner. Did you know that we seem to be hardwired to remember negative experiences more than positive ones? It's true. Science suggests that as humans evolved, it was important for them to remember the things that caused them pain or harm so that they could figure out how to either avoid the situation or handle it so it did not cause distress in the future. This is why we may have a fantastic day with our partner—a day full of love, laughter, and happiness— and it can be totally destroyed by *one* negative interaction.

Now that you have an idea as to why we remember negative experiences so well, it should be easy to understand why it is important to act loving toward your partner even when you don't really want to. Of course, no one is perfect and slip-ups can and will occur, but the quality of your relationship will improve dramatically if you make an effort to be kind and loving toward your partner even when it is difficult to do so.

When you don't have loving words to share, loving acts will go a long way.

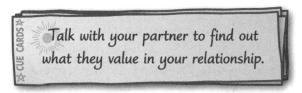

★ CUE CARDS ★

Talk with your partner to find out what they value in your relationship.

When we're in a healthy love relationship, we usually try to make our partner happy. When we're able to do this, it usually brings us joy. One of the more common problems I see in my work with clients is that couples seem to have difficulty really *knowing* what makes their partners happy. One well-intentioned partner may do something to show their love for the other, yet for some reason the recipient doesn't seem satisfied. He or she may wonder, "Why does my partner keep trying to give me *X* when what I really want is *Y*?" Then the partner who is making the effort is often left feeling that nothing they do makes their spouse happy. It kind of seems like a dog chasing its tail, doesn't it?

You would be very surprised to learn how many people tell me that they never really talk to their partners about the things they want from the relationship. The flip side of this, of course, is that many people tell me they expect their partners to "just know" what makes them happy. Exactly how is anyone supposed to "just know"?

Let me share a story about a couple I know that was a living example of this . . .

Meagan and Steve have been friends of ours for a very long time. To me, and to our mutual friends, it has always been evident that Meagan and Steve are very much in love. One day I went out to lunch with Meagan. We got to talking about our husbands and she confided in me that although she loved Steve deeply, she felt there was a growing distance in their relationship. At first I had difficulty believing her, but as she continued to speak I could tell that she was really sad and hurt by the lack of connection she sensed between them.

She told me Steve was only physically affectionate toward her when he wanted sex. "But he seems to adore you," I said. "He takes you wherever you want to go, and if you so much as hint at anything you like, he gets it for you."

"That's just it," Meagan said. "He gets me anything I want, but honestly if he would just come up behind me, kiss me on the neck, and tell me I'm beautiful, I'd rather have that than anything else."

"Have you ever told him that?" I asked.

"Well, not directly," she says.

"So how is he supposed to know?" I asked.

She sighed and said, "I guess you're right, Christina."

"Look," I said, "I don't want to tell you what to do, but I think you should let him know how you feel. He gives you anything you want. I'm sure if he knew how important this was to you, he'd be much more affectionate."

A few months later, when my husband and I were having dinner with Steve and Megan, Steve said, "I want to thank you, Christina."

"For what?" I asked.

"You've saved me a fortune," he replied.

"Huh?"

"Meagan told me what you two talked about when you had lunch a few months ago, and after all this time, if I'd known she just wanted me to touch her more often, I could have saved a fortune in jewelry."

Meagan added, "After our lunch I told him what I really wanted from him, and it worked. Steve said he thought he was showing his affection by what he was buying me, so all this time we had this crossed-signal thing going. Now that he knows what's more important to me, I'm happier and he's happier, so thank you."

See what I mean? All this time Steve was doing what he thought Meagan wanted (buying her expensive gifts), yet he didn't know what she *really* wanted. Certainly, the disconnect was not entirely Steve's fault—Meagan was never clear about expressing her desires and seemed to hope things would somehow just magically get better.

Communication does not happen magically in a relationship. It takes time and effort to communicate with your partner, and it has to happen on a regular basis. Talk *with* your partner and find out what they value in your relationship. It's the only way you will know for sure.

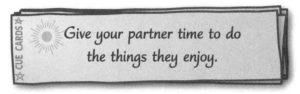

CUE CARDS

Give your partner time to do the things they enjoy.

While it is important in relationships to have some common interests, there is nothing wrong with each member of a couple having *separate* interests. Think about it: When you originally met, the two of you had your individual interests, and then you developed interests as a couple. I think individuals often feel they need to share all of their partner's interests. This is a very unrealistic expectation, of both your partner and yourself. While perhaps your common interests played a part in drawing you to one another, this does not mean you must entirely give up activities you enjoy if your partner doesn't like them. You may like scrapbooking and loathe camping—and the opposite may be true for your partner. The things we enjoy doing as individuals make us who we are.

Allowing our partner to be the person they want to be demonstrates how much respect we have for our partner and

how much we value them as a person. When we make it difficult for them to do the things they like to do, or try to get them
to only like what we like, we are in essence telling our partner that their likes and dislikes are not important. Of course,
if your partner has a penchant for strip clubs or high-stakes
gambling, it is probably unrealistic for them to think that you
will be supportive of these activities. But within reason it is
important to encourage your partner to be who they really
are, not who you think they should be.

Avoid nagging or laying a guilt trip on your partner when
they are doing something they enjoy. If you have encouraged
your partner to participate in an activity—or even a *non*activity—they like, then complaining about it sends a mixed message. It can spoil their fun and take away the positive feelings
you created by accepting their desire to enjoy themselves in
their own way.

When you accept your partner for who they are, they are
unlikely to shut down emotionally, which often happens when
individuals feel they need to keep giving up parts of themselves in order to make a relationship work.

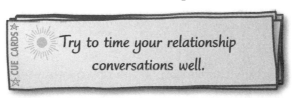

CUE CARDS

Try to time your relationship
conversations well.

When it comes time to have a serious discussion about an issue in your relationship, as discussed in Chapter 1, timing is everything. If your partner is not in the mood to talk and/or is distracted by another circumstance demanding his or her attention, it is unlikely you will be able to have a meaningful and productive conversation. As mentioned in the previous card, no one likes to be nagged or cajoled into something, even if it's something they want to do. In general, the more you push someone to talk, the less likely the person will be inclined to do so.

While it's important to discuss your relationship with your partner from time to time, it is just as important to time the conversation so that your partner will be able to hear what you have to say and give it their full, productive attention.

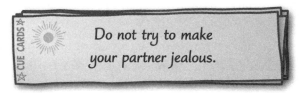

Do not try to make your partner jealous.

In my practice and in life, I have often seen couples who seem to make it a sport to make each other jealous. Then they complain that their partner is either possessive or insecure. It's almost as though the instigating partner fails to see their own role in creating this problem. If you are in a committed relationship and still checking out others or sending flirtatious messages to someone other than your partner, you may want to ask yourself why.

In my experience, the person who tends to stir up the jealousy is typically the one with the problem. If you are secure and content with yourself, there is no reason to continually seek the affirmation of others to the detriment of your primary love relationship. If you are insecure, it's probably time to look within yourself to figure out what you feel is lacking in your life and take steps to fix it. If you truly love your partner, making them jealous will not bring the two of you any closer.

A couple that plays together stays together.

Shared experiences are a great way for couples to keep their love alive. When couples play together, they are able to take a break from their day-to-day routine and interact with one another in a light-hearted, nonsexual way reminiscent of their early courtship days. Physical activity is one kind of play. Offer to go for a walk, hike, or bike ride, or find some type of exercise you can do together or a recreational sport you both enjoy. Consider joining a gym as a couple. Help each other get moving. An additional benefit of an activity-based shared experience is that exercise often helps reduce feelings of stress.

Stress can wreak havoc in partnerships by making us irritable, and it can also skew our perspective on our relationship by making minor problems seem much worse than they are. Keeping stress at bay can have a huge impact on each partner's individual happiness and in turn on the overall health of the relationship.

If the two of you prefer indoor activities, try bonding experiences like visiting museums, attending music concerts, and going to the theater, or board games like chess, checkers, and backgammon. One of the fondest memories I have from my honeymoon is playing a game of chess with my husband on our hotel balcony. Lighthearted roughhousing and pillow fights are also fun. The activities you choose don't need to be expensive; they just need to be something both of you enjoy.

Shared recollections also give couples something to talk about later as they reminisce about the good times. If a partnership hits a rough patch, happy memories can help the pair get things back on track by reminding them that they are indeed capable of having positive experiences together.

CUE CARDS

Take care of your appearance — not only for your partner but, more importantly, for yourself.

After some years of marriage and after the kids come along, it can be easy to let your appearance slide—and this is true for both women *and* men. Women, you don't need to look like a supermodel for your partner to continue to find you attractive, but you should make at least some effort to take care of your appearance. If you've gained some weight, work on trying to slim down (also important for your own health). If your wardrobe consists of shapeless, baggy clothes, add a pair or two of well-fitting jeans and a couple of flattering tops you can wear on the weekend, when you tend to spend more time with your partner. At the same time, when you look in the mirror don't be too hard on yourself if you are not a size two. Remember, studies show that women think men find the ultra-thin look attractive, but in fact men tend to favor women who have a little meat on their bones. If you are well-groomed and put a bit of effort into your appearance, you will feel better about yourself and your partner will notice. Confidence is always sexy.

This advice also applies to men. While men are supposedly more visually oriented than women, women on the whole still seem to appreciate a man who puts a little effort into his appearance. Most women I have met don't require their partners to have six-pack abs and be perfectly manscaped, but they do appreciate it when their man looks presentable. Men, if you pay attention to your appearance by maintaining a healthy weight and good grooming, the woman in your life will appreciate it and most likely will feel more sexually attracted to you. Most men like sex, and if skipping an occasional beer and burger could mean more sex, would you make the sacrifice? Something tells me you would. Again, neither partner needs to have a perfect physique, but a healthy, well-groomed, and clean appearance will usually go a long way.

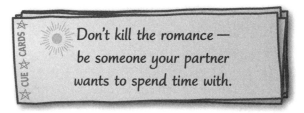

CUE ☆ CARDS ☆

Don't kill the romance — be someone your partner wants to spend time with.

If you have a tendency to be critical of everything your partner does or to nag your partner about all the things they don't do, it will eventually become hard for your partner to have romantic feelings for you. Who wants to be around someone who's always negative? With all of life's challenges, it may be hard to avoid seeing everything in a negative light, but try to remember that you and your partner are a team. Keeping a positive tone to the relationship will help you face life's challenges together with greater resolve and will also increase your romantic feelings toward one another.

Compliment
your partner generously.

When you notice something good about your partner, compliment them on it. You may think your partner knows how you feel and that the words do not need to be spoken, but in fact they do need to be spoken. No one is a mind reader. If your partner looks great, say so. If they have done something you really appreciate, let them know. If your partner is a stay-at-home parent, keep in mind that they don't get a job evaluation for how they're doing, nor do they have the opportunity to work with others and receive acknowledgment for all their hard work. No matter who you are or what your circumstances are, a compliment or acknowledgment is always nice to hear and helps you feel good about yourself. Make a rule to give your partner at least two compliments for every complaint you have; your relationship will be much, much happier.

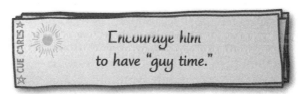

Encourage him
to have "guy time."

While it's socially acceptable for women to have "me time," the same is not always true for men. For some reason, it seems men are discouraged from hanging out with other men and are expected to go home and "spend more time with the wife and family." These days, we expect men and women to have equal amounts of responsibility in relationship and household duties, but we don't seem to encourage men to take care of themselves in the same ways we encourage women to.

The happiest couples appear to be those who maintain balance in their respective career, household, relationship, and interpersonal responsibilities. If it's been a while since the man in your life has spent time with his buddies, encourage him to do so. Balance is good for women *and* men.

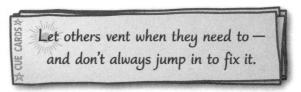

CUE CARDS

Let others vent when they need to — and don't always jump in to fix it.

Sometimes when people have had a difficult day or feel frustrated about something or someone, they like to process their feelings by venting to their partner. When your partner is venting, your natural inclination may be to jump in and help to fix the situation. This isn't always a good idea. If you're wondering whether or not your partner wants help with a problem, just ask. People are usually really good at telling you what they need when they're asked. And if your partner replies, "I'm just venting," take their word for it and let them continue.

Giving your partner the opportunity to talk about their frustrations lets them know that you are emotionally supportive.

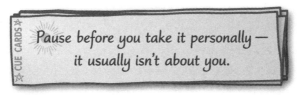

This Cue Card takes practice, but if you are able to master it you will learn an incredible amount about your partner. You will also be able to transfer this skill to other areas of your life. As feeling individuals, we tend to personalize others' actions toward us. If someone does something that offends us, we tend to think, "They did that to be mean or to hurt my feelings." What I would like you to do next time you feel this way is to pause before you react. I know from personal experience that it's a very hard thing to do, but try to control your impulse to respond automatically. Instead, stop and think about whether your partner acts this way with anyone else.

Let me illustrate. I had a couple in my office and the wife shared with me how much she disliked going places with her husband because, true to the stereotype, when they got lost he absolutely refused to ask for directions. They were ending a trip to Las Vegas and planned to stop at a shoe store where they usually spent their winnings on their way out of town. For some reason on this trip they could not find the shoe store.

Fuming as though she were reliving the experience, she told me, "Christina, we drove round and round in Las Vegas for *five* hours and he REFUSED to stop and ask for directions! He *never* asks for directions when he's lost." She felt her husband didn't care about her feelings because he knew how much she hated the wasted time, but he continued to drive around—seemingly deaf to her requests—and to remain focused on "magically" finding their destination. Then she added, "He never gets lost when he's alone." I asked her how she knew that, to which she replied, "Well, he never tells me he gets lost, and I just know he doesn't."

I asked the husband if it was true that he never got lost on his own. He said, "I always get lost, I just don't tell her about it." The wife looked surprised. And so it was revealed that this husband simply had a poor sense of direction. He recounted a story from his college days about how he took four and a half hours to drive his buddies to the beach because he made a wrong turn and ended up in the mountains before he realized he was going the wrong way. His friends told him they were tired and wanted to go back to their dorm, but he insisted that they "complete the mission," and so they did, finally getting to the beach at 2:30 in the morning. I said to the wife, "See? He's not just insensitive to you, he's like that to everyone. He's been that way since college."

While it was not okay that the husband was insensitive about the issue, what made his actions more understandable, and perhaps even somewhat tolerable, was the fact that his insensitivity was not directed solely at his wife. A few sessions later the wife told me that now when they got lost and he refused to ask for directions, she didn't get as angry as she used to because she understood that her husband's actions weren't directed toward her. To be proactive, she now prints out directions before they go anywhere, and she is planning to get him a GPS for his next birthday.

Sometimes, when we gain a better understanding of a problem, it helps us feel less frustrated. When we're able to step back and gain a better perspective, we usually become more skilled at finding solutions. I encourage you to take this skill even farther and practice it with others besides your partner. I think you will soon find that misunderstandings with most of the other people you know will be less intense and will not last as long.

✩ Cue Cards for Arguments and Disagreements ✩

For the times when tempers start to flare, here are Cue Cards that will help you improve the tone and quality of your arguments and keep your disagreements from becoming bigger than they need to be.

Ask yourself:
How important is this argument?

Before you engage in an argument, try to stop for a moment and ask yourself, "How important is this?" Of course, that's much easier said than done, but if you can do it, the quality of your arguments will improve. What I mean is that your arguments will be shorter in duration and will more likely lead to a mutually acceptable resolution. The number of arguments you have will most likely decrease as well. In the heat of the moment it's hard to look clearly at things that make us angry, but if you can take ten minutes to reflect on the issue, your overall relationship with your partner will improve. Not all arguments are worth having, and you will be wise to pick your battles carefully.

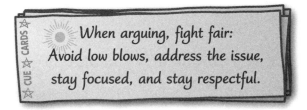

When arguing, fight fair:
Avoid low blows, address the issue,
stay focused, and stay respectful.

When we are angry at someone we love, it is very common to lash out and say things to hurt our partner because *we* feel hurt. Hurtful things said and done during the heat of an argument can leave long-lasting scars in even the best relationships, so it's important to gain control of your impulses and refrain from being intentionally hurtful. I call this "fighting fair." If you can master this skill, you will spend a lot less time arguing and do less damage to your relationship.

I also tell couples to address the issue, not the person. Let's say your wife runs late every time the two of you go anywhere together. Maybe you're in the habit of saying, "I'm sick of this! You're always late, and we always end up arguing before we go out because you can't get it together!" Instead, try this: Calmly ask your wife, "What can I do in the future to help you be ready on time?" See how this is different? It's basically removing the word "you" and replacing it with "I." I encourage you to try this approach. It helps take the personalization out of your arguments, and by staying issue-specific you avoid making the argument larger than it needs to be. If the problem is being late, address the tardiness—don't attack the person.

When it comes to fighting fair, it is extremely important to remember not to bring up past issues. When couples bring old issues into new arguments, it's usually a recipe for disaster. Stay focused and stay respectful. Remember, this is the person whom you supposedly love. If you would not let another person speak to your partner disrespectfully, you shouldn't either.

Lastly, it also helps to approach an argument from the perspective that *you* may have done something to contribute to the problem. Just a thought.

> *Try to keep family and friends out of your serious arguments, and if you do involve them, don't bad-mouth your partner.*

Unfortunately, many couples involve outsiders in their arguments. If you have a disagreement, argument, or fight with your partner, avoid sharing the intimate details about it with your neighbors, friends, or family. While all of us need emotional support during a rough spell, be careful about what you tell others, and always aim to do so without bad-mouthing your partner. A lot of couples seem to forget that the people they share these details with will remember them long after everything is resolved between the two partners. Also, doing this encourages outsiders to bring up their own agendas, take sides, meddle, and steer the disagreement toward an outcome *they* would want and not necessarily one *you* would want. If you need support during an argument with your partner and can't get it without criticizing him or her, you will most likely be better served seeking the support of a neutral third party, someone who doesn't know you and your partner as a couple.

Support groups and clergy can provide this kind of support either for free or at a very low cost.

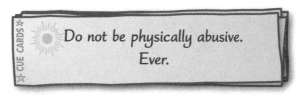

Do not be physically abusive. Ever.

If you have difficulty expressing your anger without being verbally abusive or physically violent, the truth is that you should not be in an intimate relationship. It is *never* okay to hit, slap, kick, bite, or in any other manner hurt, threaten, or intimidate another person when you are angry or frustrated. It is also never acceptable to destroy another person's property, regardless of how angry you are at them. If you are unable to express your anger, frustration, hurt, or any other emotion without resorting to violence or destruction of property, please seek help from a licensed mental-health professional. Don't be ashamed or embarrassed about seeking professional help to assist you in learning how to express your emotions without violence and destruction. You will have much healthier relationships of all kinds when you learn to express yourself without harming others.

If you are the victim of domestic violence, immediately call the police. Also, please consider seeking the assistance of a licensed mental-health professional to help you learn how to select emotionally healthier romantic partners. If you're in an abusive relationship, please see the Resources section at the end of this book for websites and phone numbers to assist you in getting the help you or your partner needs. No one who cares about you should *ever* physically hurt you.

Cue Cards for for Nurturing Your Relationship

Now let's look at some Cue Cards that you can use "behind the scenes"—things you can do that your partner may not even be aware of but that will enormously benefit your relationship.

CUE CARDS

Help your partner
look good in public.

Whenever you are out with your partner in public—at a restaurant, a party, a business function, even grocery shopping—do your best to make your partner look good. Making your partner look good includes taking care of your own appearance so *you* look good, and, more importantly, demonstrating to others how much you really care about your partner. You can do this by practicing good social skills and treating your partner with dignity and respect. For example, if your partner is doing something that bothers you or that you are critical of, take him or her aside at a time and in a way that is not obvious to others and whisper in his or her ear what you are bothered by or concerned about.

Have you ever witnessed one member of a couple loudly criticizing the other in public? I think people sometimes forget that what they find offensive in their partner may go unnoticed by others. Criticizing your partner in public not only makes him or her feel bad; it also draws attention to the perceived problem. Keep in mind that others see you interact as a couple in public for a limited time. If they observe you criticizing your partner, nitpicking, or otherwise treating her or him with disrespect, they may think your relationship is like that all the time. If you demonstrate that you like and respect your partner when you're in public, others will perceive your relationship in a good light.

Like it or not, our partner's behavior can influence how others view us. If one partner treats the other poorly, others may think the ill-treated partner has low self-esteem or is being abused. Likewise, if one partner treats the other with dignity and respect, outsiders will see the couple as happy and emotionally intact. If you find yourself being critical of or demeaning your partner in public, work on addressing the issues you have with him or her respectfully and in private.

By making your partner look good—by being on your best behavior when your partner needs you to be—you show that you care and respect their feelings, and you send the message that you are looking out for his or her best interests. When you are the person your partner needs you to be on a consistent basis, it reinforces the feeling that "we are in this together" and strengthens you as a couple.

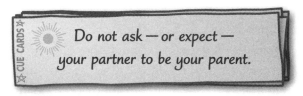

Do not ask — or expect — your partner to be your parent.

CUE CARDS

It is not your partner's responsibility to act as your surrogate parent. If you have a habit of getting yourself into trouble and needing your partner's assistance to get out of it, the romantic feelings your partner has for you will eventually diminish and change. He or she may still love you, of course, but it won't be the type of love that mates feel toward each other; it will be more like a parent/child relationship.

To keep the romantic feelings alive in your relationship, I urge you to avoid putting your partner in the parental role or placing him or her in the position of regularly having to make excuses for your behavior. Take care of yourself as any reasonable adult would, and be responsible for your own actions.

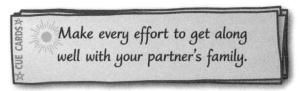

Make every effort to get along well with your partner's family.

In general, women tend to be closer to their family of origin then men do. This means a man will often end up spending more time with his wife's side of the family—for example, sharing holidays, birthdays, and the like. Although you do not have to be best friends with her relatives, it would be a loving gesture for you to make a genuine attempt to get along with them. Be courteous and respectful during visits—as you would like your partner to be when she interacts with *your* family. If someone in your partner's family is making it consistently difficult for you to be cordial, address it with your partner *in private*, and let him or her address it with the offending person. If resolution cannot be found, discuss with your partner how to effectively handle it, and if your strategies do not work and the problem persists, discuss ways that you can politely minimize contact.

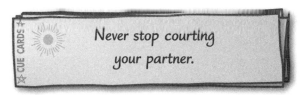

Never stop courting your partner.

Flirting with your partner needn't end once you are in a committed relationship. Leave a short "I love you" note in a place where you know she or he will find it. Bring home flowers for the heck of it. Thoughtfulness is one of the key ingredients in healthy relationships, and I've never met a person who failed to appreciate a partner's loving attention.

3 Marriages, Babies, In-Laws, and All Things Family

*E*ngagements, weddings, births, graduations, deaths — these are all milestones that we experience either directly or through a friend or relative. At these events, families usually gather to celebrate or mourn. Although the events differ, one feature they share is that they are times of stress. The stress may be positive or negative, but it is stress nonetheless. There is the pressure of trying to create the perfect wedding day or of hoping a birth will go smoothly. There is the stress experienced by a new mother and father as they think about their responsibility to be good parents to their child. There's the strain that comes with the grief we feel when we lose someone near to us. Basically, when there are changes in life, we experience stress as we adjust to the new circumstances. The stress can either help us or hinder us, depending on how we react to it. It may help us learn to handle uncomfortable situations better, or it may detract from our performance by rendering us somehow emotionally or socially less effective. Often adding to our stress is the fact that others around us are also experiencing stress in reaction to the event.

In a perfect world, when families and friends came together to observe milestones, everyone would be happy to see each other and things would go smoothly. In reality, however, some individuals handle the stress better than others. Some overreact, some behave insensitively, some seem to become downright annoying. This chapter offers Cue Cards for major life transitions. If you find yourself feeling stressed out about family events, or if you know of someone who struggles during them, read and share the Cue Cards that follow to help you feel more at ease.

☆☆☆ Cue Cards for New Couples ☆☆☆

Engagements and weddings are among the happier life events, but they are very often clouded with hurt feelings, turf wars, and arguments. Perhaps it is the melding of two families and their traditions that causes the clash, or perhaps the new in-laws just don't like their son's or daughter's choice of a spouse, but it is fairly common for a wedding to be burdened with unhappy feelings.

This section and the next one focus on how you can help the launching of a new couple be a happier, lower-stress time for all parties involved. This section is addressed to the couple, and the one that follows is for the parents.

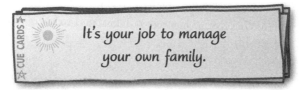

It's your job to manage your own family.

When I do premarital counseling with couples, one of the most important things we work on is each spouse managing their own family. Your spouse is new to your family, and the simple truth is that many families have difficulty accepting new people into their family system. Sometimes families will pick on the new spouse, or some family members may be downright hostile and reject him or her. Even in well-adjusted and accommodating families, social slipups can and will occur. I always try to prepare couples for the inevitable fact that at some point the new spouse will have their feelings hurt in some way by their partner's family. Also, while it is reasonable to hope that, given time, even the least welcoming families will open up to the "new" member, sometimes that does not happen. When it doesn't, your spouse may start to resent you for failing to stand up on her or his behalf.

What do I mean by "manage your family"? If you have a relative who acts in a hurtful manner toward your spouse, even if it is very subtle, it is *your* responsibility to address the issue with the offending family member, and, if warranted, to ask that person to apologize to your spouse. I am convinced that if more couples would follow this Cue Card, many arguments (and perhaps some divorces) could be prevented. When you manage your family, you show respect for your spouse, and you demonstrate through your actions that you care for his or her well-being. You minimize resentments your spouse may have about your family's behavior, strengthen the bond of your marriage, and help define your boundaries as a couple.

CUE ☆ CARDS ☆

Resolve your relationship problems directly with your partner, and try to leave your family out of it.

Disagreements are a normal part of any relationship. When you have a disagreement with your spouse, one of the best things you can do for your marriage is *not* to talk about it with your family of origin. Families can be a wonderful source of support, but in new relationships it is important for a couple to establish an identity that is separate from their respective familiesPart of establishing this identity is learning to resolve conflicts without involving family members. When you resolve a conflict directly with your spouse, you strengthen your ability to work together in making decisions that are best for the two of you. You engender trust in one another and minimize the possibility of creating feelings of resentment in your spouse or your family of origin, which often happens when one party feels as though you are "taking sides."

Think about it: If you tell certain family members about every disagreement you have with your spouse, they will quickly get the impression that you are in a bad relationship and they will start to see your spouse in a negative light. Conversely, your spouse, during disagreements, will begin to feel your stance is being influenced by your family, creating a no-win situation for all involved. Your family should only know what you choose to share with them, and you would do best for your relationship, your family, and *yourself* to keep your family's general impression of your spouse positive.

CUE CARDS

Establish your own family traditions with your partner.

New couples usually bring traditions from their families of origin into their relationship. In addition, some couples establish their own traditions. This is a normal and healthy part of any marriage. Where problems seem to occur is when families of origin insist the couple continue to follow *their* traditions and are unwilling to accommodate anything different. Typically, when problems about traditions do arise, it seems to be around how, when, and with whom holidays will be celebrated.

What I suggest is to alternate most holidays between families and perhaps choose one holiday in the year to establish your own tradition. This accomplishes three things. First, each family gets the same amount of holiday time with the couple. Next, the couple isn't stressed out and exhausted by having to travel hours and hours between two (or more) locations. Lastly, it gives the new couple the opportunity to establish a tradition and style of their own, which helps them define their identity as a couple. (My husband and I use this system and find it to be very effective.) Close-knit families sometimes have difficulty accepting the new couple alternating holidays, but in time, as with most patterns of behavior, it will become normal.

✩✩ Cue Cards for Parents and In-Laws ✩✩

If you are the parents of a new couple, you will have a more positive relationship with them if you respect their traditions *and* their boundaries. Basically, your task is to show them the respect you would any other adults. Sometimes this can be difficult. The Cue Cards that follow can help ensure that your relationship with your adult children will transition smoothly from one stage of life to the next.

> **CUE CARDS**
> Do not make negative comments about your child's choice of marriage partner.

If you had a very close relationship with your adult child prior to his or her marriage, it is quite natural that you will miss the close bond you shared and at times even feel sad about it. In time, though, the feelings of sadness will pass as you readjust your relationship to accommodate your new family member, the spouse of your adult child. As you work to make this transition, avoid saying negative things about your son- or daughter-in-law. Snide remarks about your child's new spouse will damage your relationship with him or her and could lead to a total cutoff between you and your child. Relationships between husband and wife can be difficult enough in the beginning; refrain from being a trouble-making third party.

CUE CARDS

Respect your
adult child's decisions.

You raised your son or daughter to be capable of making his or her own decisions. Now that he or she is married, you may not always agree with the choices the new couple makes. I cannot stress enough that if you want to maintain an ongoing and pleasant relationship with your child and their spouse, keep your opinions to yourself and refrain from meddling. Married couples do not need their parents scrutinizing and commenting on their every move. Perhaps your daughter has chosen to move out of state to pursue a career opportunity, or maybe your son and his wife are raising their children differently from how you did it. Part of your role as a parent is to make the transition from being the mother or father of a child to being the mother or father of an *adult*. Adults have their own opinions, interests, and feelings. They also have critical-thinking skills, which they use to form their own opinions, interests, and feelings. They no longer need your oversight. You have had your opportunity to live your life and raise your children in the way you saw fit; now it is your son's or daughter's turn to do the same. Let them have it.

> ☆ CUE CARDS ☆
>
> Respect your adult child's
> boundaries and independence.

Always aim to treat your adult child and her or his spouse in the manner you wish to be treated: with dignity and respect. (They, in turn, will probably treat you the same.)

Unannounced visits or demands to spend time together are simply disrespectful. If you would like to see your child and their spouse, call first, and see if you can arrange a time to get together. When you do visit their home, don't snoop, rearrange their belongings, or criticize their housekeeping. This is their home, not yours, and it is important to always be respectful of that fact. After all, you would not want your new son- or daughter-in-law going through your things or commenting that your housekeeping skills are not up to par, would you?

Well-meaning parents, regardless of their adult child's age, often feel inclined to offer advice on seemingly trivial issues to a newly married couple. Unless there is a life-threatening situation at hand, as much as you would like to add your perspective, refrain from doing so unless you are asked. Navigating life's issues on their own and establishing a home as husband and wife helps couples grow.

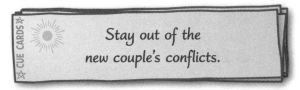

*Stay out of the
new couple's conflicts.*

All relationships have their ups and downs, and eventually all couples will argue. If your son or daughter comes to you to discuss an argument they have had with their spouse, redirect them to resolve it directly with their spouse and ask to be left out of it. Though your intentions of offering emotional support may be good, things could backfire very quickly if the other spouse feels betrayed that their husband or wife confided intimate details of the relationship to mommy or daddy. Encourage your adult child to use their problem-solving skills to get through differences with their spouse; this is part of being a good parent to your adult child. Doing this encourages your child to improve his or her conflict-resolution skills and sends the message that you support and respect your child's marriage. In addition, you avoid being put in the middle of an argument, which is never a good place to be. Stay out of it, and you will be happy you did.

*Be a good grandparent to your
grandchildren, and don't undermine
your children's authority as parents.*

The most important aspect of being a good grandparent is to avoid undermining the parents. Be respectful of rules and schedules the parents have in place for their children, and do not try to "sneak" anything past the parents even "just one time." Despite any feelings you may have about the parents being overly strict, it is not your place as a grandparent to relax any rules that are in place. When you honor the wishes of the parents, you help build their trust in you, which may lead to their permitting you to spend more time with your grandchild without their presence. This means abiding by rules regarding allowable activities, permitted foods, bedtime schedules any rule the parents have asked you to observe. Remember, in most states, having access to your grandchildren is a privilege and not a right. You will protect that privilege much better if your grandchild's parents can trust that you will not undermine them.

✩✩ Cue Cards for Pregnancy and Birth ✩✩

Now, let's look at some Cue Cards that will help you be a good grandparent *before* the baby arrives. I cannot begin to tell you how many people get hurt feelings over the birth of a child. In fact, it is not all that unusual for family problems to start brewing when a couple simply *announces* a pregnancy. Everyone is excited about the forthcoming child, and everyone seems to have an opinion about every aspect of the pregnancy experience. I once witnessed a mother-in-law say to her very pregnant daughter-in-law, "If the baby comes out being a girl, I'm going to stuff it back in until it comes out a boy!" (This exchange is a clear example of how things could have started off on a very bad footing, but the daughter-in-law handled it with dignity and grace, saying, "The only thing that is important to me is that my baby is healthy.")

I don't have children, but I have counseled enough pregnant women to know that sometimes the hormones released during pregnancy and soon afterward can cause a woman to be a little more sensitive than usual, making it difficult to overlook the insensitive comments of others. If you are expecting a baby, below are some Cue Cards to share with your family members to help them help *you* through your pregnancy.

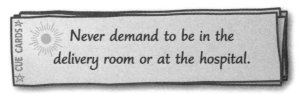

CUE CARDS ★   *Never demand to be in the delivery room or at the hospital.*

This is a huge one. Many, many couples struggle over how to handle different family members' demands during the birthing process. The birth of a child is a unique and special time for the mother and father, and it is also a medical event.

Regardless of your relationship to the couple, it is inappropriate to ask to be in the birthing room. I stress the phrase "regardless of your relationship to the couple" because some relatives tend to believe that because they are "family" or "close family," there should be a different set of standards for them than for other relatives and friends.

In most cases, a great deal of tension and unhappiness could be eliminated if all family members respected the boundaries and wishes of the parents. No matter how close you are to the mother or father, avoid trying to impose your will in this matter. If the mother wants you there, she will let you know. Some women love to share the birthing experience; others prefer to have only physicians and nurses in the room. Whatever the birthing mother desires and is comfortable with should be respected.

If you are a well-meaning grandparent who is excited about the birth of your grandchild, that is wonderful, but please keep in mind that the birthing mother's wishes should receive top priority. You will have plenty of opportunity to cuddle with your grandbaby later, but I can just about promise you that the amount of time you get to spend with your grandchild in the future will be directly related to how well you respected the mother's wishes during the birth. Remember, the health of the mother and the baby is the highest priority during a birth—not who does or doesn't get invited to witness it. Also, let's face it, people try to please friends and family members whom they *like*, so your best bet is to stay on the likable side.

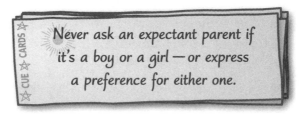

CUE ☆ CARDS ☆

Never ask an expectant parent if it's a boy or a girl — or express a preference for either one.

People often ask or express a preference about the gender of an unborn child in a lighthearted or playful fashion, but many expectant mothers and their partners do not take it that way. The couple may have had difficulty conceiving and are thrilled to have a child, and find any questions about gender offensive. The pregnancy may have been unexpected and the couple may still be processing the fact that they are indeed pregnant. Maybe the expectant parents are aware of the gender of their forthcoming child and haven't yet decided to share it with anyone else. Who knows?

If you have a gender preference, you are better off *not* expressing it either to the couple or to anyone who may mention it to them. Regardless of your relationship to the expectant parents, the gender of their unborn child truly is none of your business, and your comments will have a high probability of offending. My advice: Keep quiet and you will be glad you did.

Avoid sharing your thoughts
about baby names
unless you're invited to.

CUE ☆ CARDS ☆

Choosing a name for a child is a very personal decision and, quite honestly, one of the privileges of being a parent. Never assume, if you are a family member or close friend, that you have a right to suggest or offer "feedback." If you have ideas for a name, or strong feelings about the name the expectant parents have chosen, keep those thoughts and feelings to yourself unless the parents ask for your opinion. You will probably avoid a whole lot of ill will between you and the parents-to-be if you exercise self-restraint and stay out of the name-choosing process unless you're asked for your input.

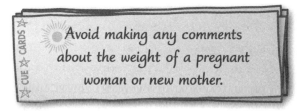

Avoid making any comments
about the weight of a pregnant
woman or new mother.

CUE ☆ CARDS ☆

Comments about the weight of others are always in bad taste, and especially so if a pregnancy is involved. That said, it is natural for pregnant women to gain weight as part of a healthy pregnancy. If a woman is struggling with her weight postpregnancy, believe me, she is well aware of it. The last thing she needs is for someone else to point it out to her. Even if a person has gained a hundred pounds since you last laid eyes on him or her, you would be wise not to comment on it.

⭐ Cue Cards for Grief and Loss ⭐

Comforting a grieving person requires a delicate balance of understanding and empathy. Let the Cue Cards below help you find that balance.

Don't try to help a grieving person by telling them stories of your own losses.

All of us have seen someone try to console a grieving person by sharing a story about how they, too, lost a loved one at some point. If this describes you, I'm sure your intentions were good, but don't do it again. Many people feel that discussing their own losses is a way to connect with a grieving person, but in reality when someone is grieving, they really don't need to hear about *other* losses. They have enough on their plate without your adding to it. This is a situation in which it is okay for the grieving person to be emotionally selfish. When someone grieves, they are in need of emotional support; be there for them and supply it.

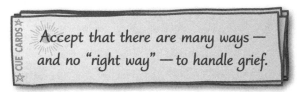

Accept that there are many ways — and no "right way" — to handle grief.

Be careful not to impose your standards on others about how grief should be handled. People deal with emotional situations differently; there is no "one-size-fits-all" approach. Just because someone responds to a loss differently from how you would does not make it wrong. When you learn to accept the individuality of others and cherish the differences between you, you will quickly begin to have less difficulty in *all* of your relationships.

Obviously, this card applies to far more than just situations of grief and loss, and it leads me to the following Cue Cards that apply to every family event, regardless of who you are or what the event is.

General Family Etiquette

Even though you can't choose your relatives, you can choose how you relate to them. Good manners will help your next family gathering go smoothly.

> ☆CUE CARDS☆ ● **RSVP** *early, arrive on time,*
> *and try not to overstay your welcome.*

When "RSVP" is mentioned in an invitation, it is a request for a response about whether or not you plan to attend. (RSVP is an abbreviation for the French phrase *Répondez s'il vous plaît*, which translates to "please respond.") It is basic courtesy to respond by the date requested. Some family and friends feel they are "so close" to the hosts that this request does not apply to them. It does. Others feel that an RSVP is only required if they plan to attend. This is incorrect. Hosts ask for an RSVP because they need to know how many people will be attending. They may have limited seating and/or want to order or prepare the correct amount of food. When you RSVP on time, you are actually helping the host plan a good party.

Sending an RSVP just two days before a planned event is not helpful. And do not take it upon yourself to RSVP for others or invite guests on behalf of the hosts. If there is someone you know who did not receive an invitation, there is probably a good reason.

Another issue that often causes tension, especially during family gatherings, is when someone doesn't arrive on time. Being punctual is simply common courtesy. If you are invited to be at an event at a certain time, be there at or close to that time. It is not only rude to your host to be late; it is also rude to other guests as they may have to wait for you so the event can proceed as planned. If you have a difficult time being punctual, one easy way to get to places on time is to set your clock, watch, or cell phone ten minutes ahead. It may sound a little corny, but it works!

Finally, as things wrap up at a party or gathering, remember not to overstay your welcome. If you're unsure about the proper time to leave, watch what others are doing. If there are a number of people leaving, then it's most likely a good time for you to leave as well.

> ★ CUE CARDS ★
>
> *Remember, it's not always about you;*
> *be willing to share the spotlight.*

Most of us have been to gatherings where there was one person who tried to get all the attention. Perhaps when you were a bridesmaid for your sister's wedding you watched your sister's mother-in-law sit solemnly in the corner, looking like she was waiting for someone to ask her, "What's wrong?" Maybe it was a dinner party where a fellow guest monopolized the conversation and talked endlessly about her or his accomplishments. No one likes an attention hog. If you want to create and maintain strong bonds to people you care for, be willing to share the spotlight and let others have their moment without drawing all the attention to yourself. You will get your chance to shine when it is *your* turn. Be a respectful and gracious guest.

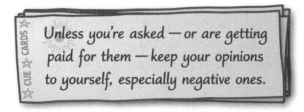

CUE CARDS

Unless you're asked — or are getting paid for them — keep your opinions to yourself, especially negative ones.

This Cue Card is really a general rule—one to live by every day. It's completely okay to have your own thoughts on things, but unless you are asked or getting paid for your opinions about someone or something, it's usually a good idea to keep those opinions, judgments, criticisms—and even witticisms—to yourself.

Cue Cards for Parents with Teens

The teen years can be difficult—both for your teen and for you as the parent. Parents tell me they don't know how to talk with their teenage children. More specifically, they complain that whatever they say, their teen won't listen. Parents ask: Do you treat them as adults or as children? One day their teen acts very mature and rational; the next day they make a completely immature decision. If you're a parent who finds yourself feeling this way, please be assured you are not alone; mood swings, mixed messages, and conflicts with parents are quite common during the teen years. One reason is because this is a time of role transition for both parent and teen. As teens struggle with establishing their independence, parents struggle with how much independence to allow. Even though there will be times when interacting with your teen may seem like it's one great big mystery wrapped in an enigma and fraught with periods of terrific volatility, that doesn't always have to be the case. The Cue Cards in this chapter will help you get a handle on how to negotiate and survive what will hopefully be your last major parenting trial.

During the teen years, adolescents are working toward establishing their own identities separate from their parents, a process that can lead to rebelliousness. In my experience and practice, I have found that there appear to be two types of parents who have the most problems with rebellious teens: parents who are very strict and authoritarian, and parents who are very lenient. When parents are too authoritarian, teens tend to feel suffocated, which in turn leads to increased acting-out behavior or, in other words, rebelliousness. Conversely, when parents are too lenient, teens may rebel because of a lack of guidance. Even when they seem to reject parental direction, in fact teens need someone to guide their behavior and tell them what is wrong—or right—with their decisions. Yes, some teens actually rebel because they *want* attention from their parents.

Let me make it clear that I think most parents do the best they can. Do parents make mistakes? Of course they do. Mine did, and yours probably did, too. The key to handling rebelliousness seems to lie in avoiding extreme parenting styles.

Another common problem between parents and teens is communication. This usually happens when parents discourage or inhibit discussions their teens may try to have with them by adopting the "I know what's best for you" approach. When a teen engages you in conversation, be open to it and don't shut him or her down. Use the golden opportunity you are being provided to listen to what they say, and to guide their decision-making skills. If your teen child is comfortable enough to engage with you in conversations about their life, I encourage you to welcome these as bonding and enriching experiences for you both.

A good way to think about how to talk with your teen is to imagine a safety zone. Remember when your child was younger and you had to monitor them closely to make sure they were safe? The safety zone you had for your young child was probably pretty small. You were most likely within a few feet of your child or otherwise pretty much knew what was going on with them almost every moment of the day. Then, as your child grew older, the safety zone got wider, and they learned about things that could hurt them. If they touched a hot stove, they'd get burned; if they ran in front of car, they'd get hit. As your child grew, you no longer had to tell them not to touch the hot stove or play in the street. In essence, you expanded your child's saftety zone, giving them more room to do things and interact with others without your supervision.

Now that your child is a teen, it's time to expand and define that safety zone again. As mentioned, parents seem to run into problems in communicating with their teen when they don't expand the safety zone. When these things happen it usually translates into the following complaints from teens:

"My parents don't listen to me."
"My parents don't understand me."

These two complaints are closely connected. If parents don't accurately and effectively listen to their teens, it's not going to be possible for parents to understand them. But to listen to your teens, you will have to have conversations with them, and that's the first challenge we'll address. To start improving your relationship with your teen, let's look at Cue Cards that will increase your odds of communicating more effectively with them.

✰✰ Cue Cards for Creating a Positive Atmosphere ✰✰

When communicating with teens, it is helpful to create a positive atmosphere. Let the Cue Cards below help you with this.

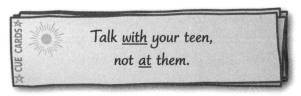

CUE CARDS

Talk _with_ your teen,
not _at_ them.

No one likes to be talked *at.*There are at least two differences between talking *with* and talking *at* someone. The first is that talking with includes asking questions and listening, rather than making statements or expressing opinions, judgments, or feelings. The second is making your questions open-ended—questions that don't simply have a yes or no answer. If you give your teen the opportunity to describe what is going on in their life rather than appearing to grill them, you will start to open up a dialogue between the two of you. Asking, "What was school like today?" will be much more effective in getting a conversation going than, "Did you pay attention in school today?" This conversational technique is actually helpful for any relationship. Closed-ended questions can put people on the defensive, no matter who it is, and they are unlikely to open up and share anything other than what is being specifically asked about. When a person feels comfortable talking with you, they are likely to tell you much more. Often, parents come to see me and complain that their teen "just won't listen to me," or "isn't interested in anything I have to say." Then, when the teen comes to see me, they tell me their parents talk down to them. As a parent, you will have much more success if you speak to your teen as you would to any adult—respectfully. Teens are not stupid, so don't treat them as if they are. And teens are not young children, so even if you are angry at your fifteen-year-old do not talk to her as if she were seven.

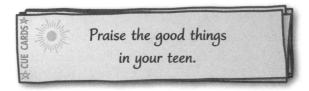

Praise the good things
in your teen.

Noticing and *commenting on* the positive things your teen does will help to shape your teen's behavior. If you point out only the negative, your teen will begin to view your words as nothing more than a constant complaint. This may lead them to rebel more because they may feel there is nothing they can do to please you. (Wouldn't you be angry with someone who criticized you all the time?) Whenever possible, make more positive than negative comments about your teen's behavior because, generally speaking, positive reinforcement is more effective than negative reinforcement.

Have dinner together
as a family.

Long work hours combined with a teen's extracurricular activities can make this difficult, but it is well worth your time and effort to have dinner together as a family at least five nights a week. Sharing an evening meal lets you reconnect with one another; it is also a very useful tool for parents to keep track of what is going on in their teen's life, which can be crucial in helping detect any problems your teen may be having. Numerous studies also indicate that teens who sit down for family meals at least five nights a week have better language skills and tend to score higher on academic achievement tests than teens who don't.

To get even more out of your family meals, include your teen in meal planning and preparation. This gives you a great opportunity to teach your teen about nutrition and the benefits of healthy eating. You can also teach them how to cook, which hopefully will lead to a decreased reliance on fast food in later life. Meal planning does not need to be difficult, nor do meals need to be expensive; simple meals of lean meats and other sources of protein along with vegetable side dishes can be easily designed to fit into any family's budget. Don't forget, you can send your teen to the market to pick up the items you need; by doing this you save yourself some time and give your teen the opportunity to learn about other parts of the store than just the snack and beverage departments.

Finally, the majority of studies conducted about family meals indicate that for them to have the most beneficial outcomes they should be pleasant in nature. If family meals become a series of lectures or arguments you will have a hard time motivating your teen to participate in them. You know the saying "You can catch more flies with honey than with vinegar"? Very true. Make family meal times an enjoyable experience for all involved to achieve true bonding. Discuss agreeable topics, talk about world affairs or local news, spend time planning the next night's meal or other family activities. Remember, the goals of this time together are to make it a positive experience for everyone and to effectively connect with your teen.

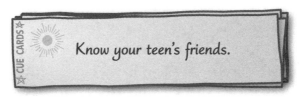

Know your teen's friends.

You don't have to like your teen's friends, but you should know who they are. In a perfect world, it is also helpful to know their parents. Teens can be heavily influenced by peer pressure. When you know your teen's friends you can help monitor his or her well-being by seeing what influences he or she is being exposed to.

Unless you have a very good reason to, it's probably not a good idea to tell your teen that you don't like one or more of their friends. Usually, it only offends the teen and may even encourage them to spend more time with the friend(s) you don't like.

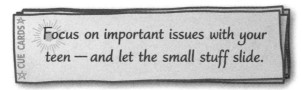

Focus on important issues with your teen — and let the small stuff slide.

If your teen is maintaining a good grade point average and is being pretty responsible with their household chores, it is probably a wise decision to avoid making an issue of it if they stay up too late sometimes. When you start micromanaging your teen's behavior, there is a good chance they will become rebellious. Very few people, including your teen, like to hear a running commentary on their every action. If your teenage son or daughter is for the most part doing what he or she is supposed to do, continue with the positive commentary on their good actions and let the little stuff slide. Your teen is an individual, after all, and that means he or she will have preferences and take actions you may not always agree with.

Cue Cards for Preventing Problems

While creating a positive environment and having family meals together will help alleviate some of the problems you may encounter with your teen, here are a few extra things you can do that should help to keep your teen (and you) on the right track.

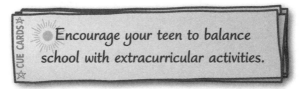

Extracurricular activities are extremely beneficial for teens. Studies have shown that teens who are involved in them have higher levels of self-esteem. Extracurricular activities augment your teen's education by giving them the opportunity to broaden their horizons. They learn new skills and discover and develop natural talents. By participating in activities such as sports, bands, glee club, or theatre groups, teens learn how to work with other people. This gives them a sense of community along with valuable team-playing and team-building skills that will benefit them throughout their adult lives.

Important as extracurricular activities are, try not to fall into a pattern that has become quite common today: Don't "overbook" your teen—be sure to leave time for those family dinners mentioned earlier.

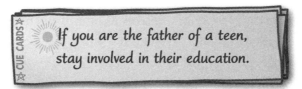

Even in this era of increasing equality between the sexes, mothers still do most of the parenting of their teens. It may be interesting to you to know that when fathers of adolescents get actively involved in their teen's life, it makes a *big* difference. Studies show that teens whose fathers are active in their education have higher levels of self-esteem, fewer behavioral problems, lower rates of substance abuse, better peer relationships, and better academic records. Also interesting is the finding that it is not the *amount* of time that a father is involved; it's the *quality* of the time. The father's involvement sends an additional message to the teen that school is important, and it does so more effectively than a lecture about the importance of school could ever do. These fathers are showing their teen the importance of school by backing their words with action.

Here are some ideas to help you fathers out there increase your involvement in your teen's schooling:

☆ Volunteer to help with the school newsletter.

☆ Participate in school fundraising opportunities.

☆ Volunteer as a class chaperone for school activities.

☆ Offer to build or maintain a website for your teen's class.

☆ Attend parent–teacher conferences.

☆ Become an active member of the PTA (Parent Teacher Association).

☆ Host a field trip to your workplace for your teen's class.

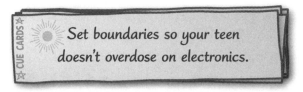

Understandably this may be a difficult task, but it is not an impossible one. Many parents of teens struggle with their teen's sleep cycle, reporting that the teen "stays up all night" and "sleeps all day." Typically, teens who do this have been up all night playing video games, chatting on social media sites, or texting friends. This seems to happen less with teens who have more structure in their lives—those who are involved in sports or other extracurricular activities or who have a part-time job. If your teen's activities all seem to be digital, it's time to get them involved in other things. Find activities for them that involve interacting with others face-to-face. This also helps them develop their in-person social skills, which are crucial to social development and career advancement in adulthood.

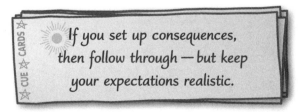

Most parents tend to establish consequences for teens who do not perform their household chores or fulfill reasonable academic and behavioral expectations. When you do this, keep in mind that for consequences to actually work, your standards and expectations need to be reasonable and suited to your child's abilities and interests. Perhaps more importantly, you need to be consistent when applying consequences. When you do not follow through, your teen learns that she or he can basically agree to anything you ask without actually doing what is expected because *you* don't. If you want your teen to take consequences seriously, you must do what you say you're going to do when expectations are not met.

If you feel guilty about having to punish your teen, keep in mind that you are helping them learn responsibility and discipline—two qualities that will be valuable for the rest of their lives.

 Cue Cards for Solving Problems

Learn to guide your teen without being overbearing, and if you are faced with a difficult problem, know when to seek additional assistance.

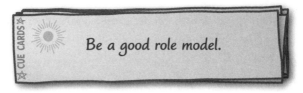

CUE CARDS

Be a good role model.

Even though you may think your teen is too old to be paying attention to the way you conduct yourself, think again. They are watching you, and they are *learning* from you. If you drink too much or have difficulty getting along with others, your teen is likely to pick up the same behaviors. If you use drugs and think your teen doesn't know about it, believe me, *they do*. If you are very materialistic, it is a little unrealistic to expect your teen to be much different. Conversely, if you are active and involved in charity organizations and community outreach programs, your teen will notice this as well and will likely follow suit in some capacity. Lastly, remember that as parents you are the primary role models for love relationships. If as parents you are verbally abusive or unfaithful to one another, your teen will learn that "this is just the way relationships are supposed to be." Conversely, if you treat each other respectfully and handle conflicts in a mature and reasonable manner, your teen will learn those skills. Children and teens are far more aware of their parents' actions than parents ever realize. The old saying "The apple doesn't fall far from the tree" is a very accurate description of what you can expect from your children, so guide them wisely through your actions.

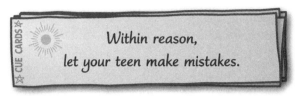

**Within reason,
let your teen make mistakes.**

As a well-meaning parent, you may be inclined to jump in and help your teen before they make a mistake. If this describes you, you are doing your teen a disservice. Part of growing and maturing is learning how to problem-solve and take responsibility for one's actions. As teens negotiate the ins-and-outs of social and peer relationships, they gain valuable life skills that will help them as adults. Though no one wants to see their children hurt emotionally by another person (e.g., by a girlfriend or boyfriend), these hurts—and the recovery from them—are a part of life. When you allow your teen to problem-solve for themselves, you let them develop the valuable trait of resilience—the ability to bounce back from life's adversities. In addition, your teen is hopefully learning insight about personal interactions and gaining an understanding of what works and what doesn't. Coping skills are essential for a well-balanced mental state, so take a step back from interfering in your teen's age-appropriate social and work situations and let him or her develop these essential life skills. Offer emotional support and productive feedback, but avoid solving their problems for them.

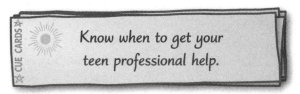

Know when to get your teen professional help.

If your teen appears to be struggling with school, drugs, or alcohol, or if your teen seems depressed or is having other behavioral issues that are becoming increasingly problematic, get them the help they need. As easy as it may seem to hope your teen "grows out of" this phase, their issues may be causing significant problems in their day-to-day functioning, and it is your responsibility as a parent to step in and help. Your teen may not initially like what you are doing, but parenting, like so much of life, is not a popularity contest. Sometimes the best decisions you can make for yourself or on behalf of others are the tough ones, so don't be afraid to do what needs to be done.

Many psychologists, marriage and family therapists, licensed professional counselors, and social workers specialize in working with teens. In addition, for more severe issues, there are treatment options that include in-patient and outpatient hospitalization programs. Your teen's school should be able to direct you toward the appropriate people to get her or him on the path to wellness. School counselors and nurses are valuable resources and are there to support the students' well-being. Ask them to steer you in the direction of getting your teen the help she or he needs.

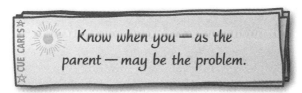

Know when you — as the parent — may be the problem.

As mentioned earlier in this chapter, teens are very aware of what goes on with their parents. If you are struggling with stress, alcohol, or drugs, or are having marital difficulties, as much as you may try to shield your teen from your issues, trust me—you can't. More often than not, behavioral issues seen in teens are due to the fact that there are problems at home. If you as the parent are having troubles and need help, please get that help—not only for your own sake but for the sake of your children. Parents are often quite surprised to see that once they resolve their own issues, the problems they were having with their kids subside. Part of being a responsible parent is to figure out when *you* are the root of the problem, and then taking action to fix it.

5 Cue Cards for Interacting with Aging Parents

*A*ging happens. No matter how much you or anyone else you know tries to stay young, aging is impossible to avoid. Though many people look, feel, and act younger than their chronological age, at some point their bodies will become frail. Some will experience declines in their reasoning and memory; others may face an age-related illness. Even if an aging adult is fortunate enough to avoid these developments, there will come a time when they require special care. In some countries, statistics indicate that the number of people living to the age of eighty and over is the fastest-growing segment of the population. There are also projections that the number of people worldwide living to the age of eighty and above will grow by as much as 233 percent between now and 2040. That is an enormous increase, and while it is a fascinating and in many cases wonderful change, the aging of our population presents many new situations that our society, and we as individuals, have never before had to deal with.

One of these situations, and perhaps one of the most difficult many of us will face, is interacting with our aging parents. We may be forced to grapple with any number of unfamiliar issues. In many cultures it is expected that adult children will care for their aging parents. What happens, though, when the children live thousands of miles away from their parents? Should the children move closer to the parents? Should the parents leave the familiarity of everything they know and move closer to their children? As adult children, how do we handle it when our aging parents do not agree with our decisions? What happens when our parents disagree with how we are rearing our own children? If we are married, what happens if we don't like our in-laws yet there is no one else to take care of them? What happens if we cannot meet our aging parents' emotional or physical needs? What happens if, for whatever reason, we don't *want* to? Conversely, as adult children, we may find ourselves growing impatient with our aging parents as they make decisions we see as not in their best interest, such as living independently when we believe it is no longer safe for them to do so, or continuing to drive when we know they should not be behind the wheel. All of these are difficult questions that have no single correct answer.

In general, by the time people reach the age at which they start exhibiting physical and cognitive decline, their adult children will range in age from their thirties to their sixties. You may be busy raising your family and pursuing a career and then find yourself with the added responsibility of making sure your aging parents are okay. This is not an easy task physically or emotionally, but if you take the time to understand your parents' new stage in life, perhaps you can develop a greater sense of compassion for them and interact with them more effectively and with less frustration.

We should remember, as we witness our parents' aging, that they are experiencing these losses firsthand. We can expect them to struggle emotionally, perhaps feeling angry or depressed, as they progressively have to give up aspects of their independence. These feelings are very normal. Put yourself in their position. If one day you woke up and were no longer able to drive your car, how would you feel? What would you do? You would have to learn to adjust to life without the convenience of your own transportation, quickly discovering that it's not so easy to have to rely on public transport. Or if you are lucky enough to have others who will transport you, you may have to deal with the worry of being a burden to them. Not being able to drive is an enormous loss of independence for many, which is why you hear stories of elderly drivers who probably shouldn't be driving getting into accidents.

Other age-related limitations can stir up feelings so strong that some elderly people will go to great lengths—sometimes recklessly so—to maintain their independence. In my years of working with aging adults and their families, family members have reported many situations in which their aging relatives were repeatedly falling in their homes or living in otherwise unsafe conditions (e.g., leaving the stove on), yet they refused to move to an assisted-living facility or to allow a family member or social-service agency to regularly check on them.

Even though there is much to be gained as one ages—such as wisdom, companionship, contentment—at some point it does become a series of losses. There is the transition from working adult to retiree, which can lead to a role transition from provider to dependent. Then one begins to outlive friends and relatives they have known forever. Another relevant issue, as surprising as it may sound to those of us under age fifty, is the advancement of technology. An aging adult may lack access to the Internet or the capacity to learn how to use all the new tools available for instant communication. This tends to lead to increased feelings of isolation.

I don't mention these issues to paint a grim picture of the aging process. My aim is to reflect reality. With all of the losses and changes seniors endure, it should not be surprising that depression is quite common. To shift to a more positive perspective, let's look at Cue Cards that can help you enhance your interactions with your aging parents.

Because of the importance—in some cases, lifesaving importance—of these Cue Cards I have also included them in the back of the book, on page 170, in the form of a checklist (I like to think of it as a "to do" list) that you can copy and keep with you for handy reference.

✯✯✯ Cue Cards for Discussions with Aging Parents ✯✯✯

There are many things we don't think about—or perhaps I should say many things we don't *want* to think about—when we think of caring for our aging parents. While some topics may be unpleasant or uncomfortable to discuss, if you are proactive in addressing key issues, you will give yourself, your parents, and the rest of your family the opportunity to resolve highly personal and often emotionally charged decisions about their care without the stress and anxiety that often happens when a crisis is imminent. Engage in caregiving conversations when all of you are of sound mind and emotionally in a good place, and you will dramatically reduce the possibility of encountering self-doubt, regret, and family arguments down the road. The Cue Cards that follow will help you open a dialogue—and hopefully create a plan—with your parents to address these essential matters.

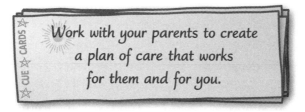

CUE ☆ CARDS ☆

Work with your parents to create a plan of care that works for them and for you.

It may not be easy to talk about aging-related issues with your parents, but I assure you it will make a difficult time *less* difficult if you discuss these matters well before it is necessary to do so. Your parents may feel uncomfortable discussing certain topics and attempt to postpone the conversation. By gently reminding them that you are concerned about their health, safety, and general well-being, you can steer the discussion where it needs to go. Also remind them that healthcare or end-of-life decisions are not entirely related to aging; accidents and illnesses can occur at any age, and it is always good to have some type of plan in place so they can make their desires known should an unfortunate circumstance occur. When you and your aging parents develop a health-related contingency plan together, you can make your own desires and concerns known, which will in many cases help reduce potential misunderstandings and conflicts down the road.

Though your relationship may be close, neither adult children nor their parents are mind readers, and making specific wants and needs known in advance will help ensure that they are met. Discussing the expectations for giving and receiving care will help keep expectations realistic for both parties and allow you to use greater understanding when approaching situations where feelings may otherwise be hurt and family rifts occur. For example, you should tell your parents if you are unable (or unwilling) to care for them if they are no longer able care for themselves. Conversely, they should tell you if they have no intention of living with you under any circumstances. Though disagreements over care arrangements and other aging-related issues may still happen, when these topics are discussed in advance both you and your parents will have the opportunity to work through conflicts.

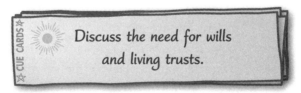

Discuss the need for wills and living trusts.

The division of a relative's—especially a parent's—assets has the potential to stir up acrimonious feelings in even the most harmonious families. During a time of heightened emotions seemingly simple decisions can erupt into turf wars very fast. Wills and living trusts help reduce the chance of conflict within a family because, ideally, they clearly state the deceased relative's desires. Not only are wills and living trusts helpful in promoting familial harmony; they are useful in protecting surviving family members against long, drawn-out actions in which the state may eventually decide how the deceased's assets will be divided.

Encourage your aging parents to create a living trust or will to protect their assets and ensure they are eventually distributed in the manner in which *they* desire. The cost of doing this varies, so it will be to your benefit to price-shop legal services. A quick search on the Internet will help you learn what is available to you. If you do not have access to a computer, ask a friend who can help you. If possible, ask your friend to print the result of their search so you will have the information handy.

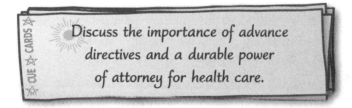

CUE CARDS ☆ ☆ ☆ — Discuss the importance of advance directives and a durable power of attorney for health care.

Discussing end-of-life decisions is never an easy task, but it is a necessary one. Many people, young and old, are unaware of the fact that if they have not made specific decisions about their health care in advance and put them in legally binding language, others *may* be allowed to step in and dictate their care if they face a critical health situation. That means they will be unable to express their wishes about treatment or issues like end-of-life care or being kept on life support. While some people may not have an issue with this, if your parent has specific desires, or has desires that you know differ from what other family members believe are needed, your parent's safest bet is to spell out the type of care they want in a legal document. Most of us hope to never encounter this problem, but in reality you don't know what can happen. Some individuals have very strong feelings about life support—either for or against. Then there are decisions about what types of measures should be pursued during end-of-life stages. Hospice? Comfort measures only? Feeding tubes? Intubation?

It has been my experience that family members making these types of decisions for their parents are already in a heightened state of emotion because they are processing their own feelings about the parent's decline in health. As a result, and due to differing perceptions about what the parent would want, bitter family arguments may ensue over what care measures should be put in place.

In a gentle manner, ask your parents if they have legal documents in place stating the type of care they would wish to receive in the event they are unable to make decisions for themselves, or if they have a legal document specifying who should make medical decisions on their behalf if they are unable to. If they have these documents in place, ask them where they are kept so that you know where to find them if and when you need them. Encourage them to keep a copy at home, or better yet, to give you a copy. If you ever need to use these documents, you will probably want to have immediate access to them, and if they are in, say, a safety deposit box, that can cause problems. If your parents haven't executed these documents, suggest that it is crucial for them to do so in order to be able to make their *own* decisions about these very personal and important issues. Then help them get the documents squared away.

✰✰ Cue Cards for Keeping Them Safe at Home ✰✰

In order to prevent some age-related accidents due to problems with balance or mobility, the next time you visit your parents, do a safety check on their home. If you don't see your parents very often, ask a sibling, other close relative, or family friend to do it. In the event your parents are sensitive about their loss of independence, the safety check can be done unobtrusively. What should you look for? The following list is by no means complete, but it's a good place to start.

> ☆ CUE CARDS ☆ Determine if your parents are having problems with balance and if there are any areas in the home that could cause them to slip or fall.

As mentioned, the elderly are more prone to broken bones and fractures as a result of slips and falls. In addition, older folks tend to have more problems with balance, which can increase the chance of a fall. Do you notice uneven flooring surfaces in their home? Small area rugs that tend to slide? If so, work with your parents to get the issues resolved in a timely manner. Also, help them install strategically placed handrails and grab bars throughout the home. These inexpensive devices are very useful when located in showers and bathtubs and near toilets, and they are readily available at most major hardware stores. Though it may not be very aesthetically pleasing, a secure, well-placed hand rail can significantly reduce the possibility of a slip or fall. Depending on the state in which your parent lives, government programs may have low-interest loans available to seniors to help cover the cost of safety modifications to their homes. Information about these types of programs, as well as other resources and benefits available to seniors and their families in the United States, may be found on the website for the Administration on Aging: www.aoa.gov/AoARoot/Index.aspx. For information about resources available for seniors in Canada, please refer to the website for the Public Health Agency of Canada: www.publichealth.gc.ca/seniors.

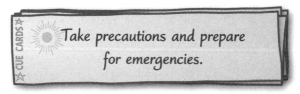

CUE CARDS ☆

☆ CUE CARDS ☆

Take precautions and prepare for emergencies.

If there is no one who can check on your parents on a regular basis, or if for some reason they prefer not to be checked on, consider setting them up with an emergency alarm, a device that is typically worn on the wrist or as a pendant around the neck. In the event of an emergency, the senior simply pushes the button on the device and a call center will dispatch or contact the appropriate emergency personnel (e.g., ambulance, fire department, police). Some systems include a feature similar to an intercom. If you are unable to reach your parent by phone and are concerned they may be in trouble, the call center will "buzz" into your parent's home via the intercom system and ask them if they are okay. If call-center staff do not receive a response, they will dispatch emergency responders to the home to assess the senior and administer needed assistance.

If you plan to hire a caregiver for your parents, ask for at least three references and then follow up on them. If the caregiver is licensed as a medical professional (e.g., a nurse, physician, etc.), most states have a licensing-board website that contains a licensee's disciplinary-action record and their license status for public viewing. A complete listing of United States Physician Licensing Board websites is available at the end of this book, in Resources. If you live in Canada, you may obtain information regarding licensed physicians through the College of Physician and Surgeons. (Please see Resources for website links to your local College of Physicians and Surgeons.)

Cue Cards for Gathering Important Information

Help yourself take better care of your parents and your parents to take better care of themselves by keeping key information handy for them. In the event of a medical emergency, the ability to provide medical treatment staff with important information about your parents on a timely basis can literally mean the difference between life and death. Let the Cue

Cards below help you and your parents be better prepared to handle everyday needs and crisis situations.

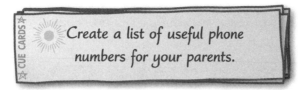

Create a list of useful phone numbers for your parents.

Place a list of useful phone numbers in a secure, visible area near your parents' phone. Be sure the writing or print is legible and a little larger than normal to help them view the information with greater ease. Include phone numbers for emergency services (911, local hospitals, physicians, fire department, police), utility companies, and friends or relatives who live close by. It may also be useful to include the phone numbers for a handyman your parents can call in the event of a home-maintenance issue and for senior transportation agencies and meal services.

Keep a copy of the names and contact numbers for your parents' physicians.

Ask your parents for the names and phone numbers of their physicians, and keep the information in a place where you will be able to find it when you need it. If your parents need to be hospitalized in an emergency, they may be unable to relay this information to the treatment staff. If you have the information you can pass it along, which may help hospital staff coordinate care and ultimately help them take better care of your parents.

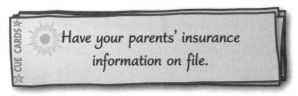

Have your parents' insurance information on file.

Almost every health-care provider requests insurance information about a patient prior to scheduling an appointment or rendering treatment. Make a copy of your parents' health-insurance information so you have it readily on hand should an emergency arise.

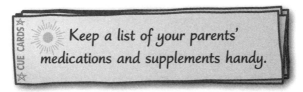

Keep a list of your parents' medications and supplements handy.

Keeping a list of your parents' medications and supplements readily available is exceptionally helpful in the event of an emergency hospitalization. If your parent is unable to speak for him- or herself, handing a list of his or her medications and supplements to the treatment team will help them understand what is going on with your parent and determine the best course of treatment. As mentioned, certain medications and supplements can have adverse effects when they interact with one another. The chances of a negative drug interaction are reduced when treatment staff are fully aware of a patient's medication and supplement regimen.

✩✩ Cue Cards for Checking Their Health Status ✩✩

The Cue Cards in this section will help you help your parents maintain a good quality of life for as long as possible by helping you to keep an eye on different aspects of their health.

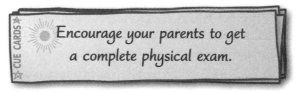

Encourage your parents to get a complete physical exam.

Although many seniors are up to date on their medical care, quite a few are not. If your aging mother or father has not had a complete physical exam in the last year, encourage them to have one. Many physical issues also affect mental alertness and mood, so make sure their physical health is attended to. For example, did you know that dehydration may cause fluctuations in mood and problems with balance? As you know, balance issues are extremely important as a person ages because falls can be devastating to older adults who have weakened bones.

During a physical exam the physician should also review your parents' medications and supplements and check to see if there are any negative drug interactions that need to be corrected. In addition, required dosages of prescription medications may change as one ages. The physician will be able to assess if the current dosage your parent is getting is appropriate.

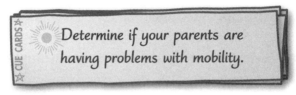

> CUE CARDS ★
>
> ● Determine if your parents are having problems with mobility.

Are your parents having difficulty moving around? Do they have problems walking, reaching, or climbing stairs? Mobility is a significant issue with aging adults because it has a direct impact on quality of life. The inability to perform simple tasks such as walking to the restroom, getting the mail, taking the dog out, and grocery shopping can become very real problems. If you notice that your parents are having mobility problems, consider mentioning it to their doctor to see what options may be available for them. Assistive devices like canes, walkers, and even scooters may be available for your parents' use, and their insurance may cover at least part of the costs of these items.

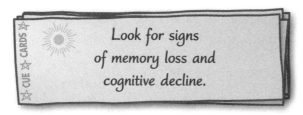

Look for signs
of memory loss and
cognitive decline.

Since your last visit, do some things look less clean or strangely out of place? For example, is there a hammer in the refrigerator? When you open a drawer, is it filled with used tissues? Uncharacteristically poor housekeeping, oddly placed items, and hoarding behaviors could indicate that a parent is experiencing a cognitive decline (a lessening of mental capacities such as perception, reasoning, awareness, and judgment). If you notice issues like these, take your parent to the doctor for a complete physical exam and evaluation. Tell the doctor about your findings and concerns. It is not uncommon for individuals with early-stage cognitive decline to minimize or deny their difficulties. You will be helping the doctor care for your parent better if you provide as much information as possible.

Cue Cards for Making Their Lives Easier

It's quite natural for most seniors to require a little extra assistance from time to time. Here are some things you can do to help make your parents' life easier and offer the "little extra" that shows that you care about them.

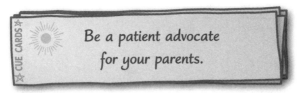

CUE CARDS

Be a patient advocate
for your parents.

If your parent is hospitalized, be an advocate for their care. This means acting as an extra set of eyes and ears to make sure your parent both (a) understands their illness and its treatment, and (b) receives the care they need. As much as we would all like to think that our loved ones will receive the best medical care possible, there are times when hospital staff are unable to attend to every patient's needs. In addition, mistakes *do* happen. If at all possible, either be present as often as you can during a hospitalization, or arrange shifts with other family members so someone stays with your parent during the hospital stay. In the event there is no family member or close friend who can help , you may want to consider hiring a private caregiver or aide who can stay with your parent during your absence. If you do hire an outside caregiver, be sure to check with the hospital regarding their policies and procedures about having a person other than family stay with your parent.

While your parent is in the hospital, you will most likely get the opportunity to meet the treating physician and be able to address any concerns directly with her or him. In addition, while the physician is talking with your parent, make note of what is being discussed so you can later go over it with your parent. It's easy for an individual to forget details or be too overwhelmed to take everything in at the moment.

During your parent's hospitalization, pay attention to their medication regimen, including what times the meds are supposed to be given. (Remember that medications may have been modified due to the change in health status.) That way, when a nurse arrives to give medications you can act as a second set of eyes to make sure there are no errors. It is also useful to keep a small journal or notebook handy in which to jot down any notes you feel are important; you can pass the notebook on to the family member who takes over at the end of your shift so they have an idea of how your parent is doing. Alternatively, create a chart and post it in a visible place for the family member or attendant to check off whenever medication is given.

Most hospitals have set visiting hours, but many people do not know that exceptions can be made. Some hospitals even have cots available for one family member to stay in the room with a patient if space permits. It is very easy for a patient to become depressed during a hospitalization for a variety of reasons—for example, not feeling well, loss of independence, boredom, worry. Having a loved one present can help alleviate some of these feelings.

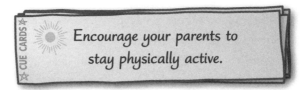

Encourage your parents to
stay physically active.

Physical activity is enormously beneficial for aging adults. Not only does it help alleviate feelings of depression; studies have shown that it may even delay or slow cognitive decline. If your parents live in an area that offers organized exercise programs geared toward seniors, encourage them to participate. If they prefer not to exercise in a group setting, encourage them to do so on their own. Walking is wonderful exercise, it is free, and it can be done just about anywhere. Studies repeatedly show that in addition to its mood-stabilizing benefits, regular exercise helps improve physical health by boosting endurance, strength, and balance.

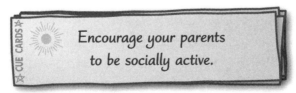

Encourage your parents
to be socially active.

Even though aging usually brings the loss of friends, encourage your parents to make new ones. Churches, parks, and community centers typically offer groups for seniors, allowing them the opportunity to socialize with their peers and participate in organized activities. Some places even offer daily lunch programs for a nominal cost. Interacting socially and connecting with others face-to-face is a wonderful antidote for depression in older adults.

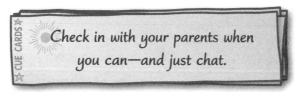

CUE CARDS

Check in with your parents when you can—and just chat.

Some elderly folks who choose to live on their own may go without contact from others for extended periods of time. If you live some distance from your parents or are very busy with work, family, or other obligations, a quick phone call once a week is a great way to "check in" with them. It can also give you an idea if they need more attention or care.

It also never hurts to call your parents for no other reason than to say hello. My master's thesis was titled *What Aging Parents Expect from Their Adult Children*. Do you know what I found? The number-one thing parents wanted was to hear from their adult children. The seniors I interviewed were not looking for anything complicated; they just enjoyed hearing from their kids once or twice a week for lighthearted chit-chat. Many aging parents never stop caring for and wanting a lifeline with their children; it is one of the most emotionally sustaining things adult children can offer them.

> **CUE CARDS**
> If you start to observe memory problems, create a memory book.

As people age, their short-term memory is often impacted. An exercise that may help is reminiscing. Many seniors have typically led a life full of colorful and interesting stories. Help your parents create a memory book. A photo album or scrap book of important people, pets, and places from their past, along with names, can help your parents recall distant memories. You can include space for them to add to it if they are capable of doing so. If you have the time, making the book with your parent can be a useful cognitive exercise for them as well as creating some bonding time for the two of you. You may find yourself enjoying hearing the old stories again, and you may hear some entertaining new ones, too. It is also okay to make the book at home and send it to your parents. Either way, the book will be very effective in stimulating your parent's long-term recall ability.

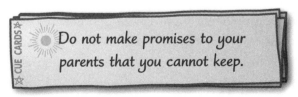

> **CUE CARDS**
> Do not make promises to your parents that you cannot keep.

Aging parents will usually have fewer commitments to occupy their time. Therefore, they tend to look forward to get-togethers and opportunities to see their adult children even if their children are just stopping by to help with a project or run errands for them. Be aware that if you say you will do something for your parents, or if you tell them you are going to stop by, they will most likely be waiting for you.

Earlier in my career, I was performing a home visit with a woman in her seventies when I noticed a rather large box under her desk. During a little lull in the conversation I asked, "What's in the box?" She told me it was a collection of books and other belongings that she no longer wanted. Her daughter had asked her to box up the items so she could take them off her hands. I asked, "How long has that box been sitting there?" She said, "Ten years. When she comes over and sees it, she always tells me she'll come back and pick it up, so I hold onto it." Put yourself in your aging parents' position: How many times have you waited for someone—be it a repairman or a perpetually late friend—only to have them fail to keep their promise to meet you when scheduled? I haven't met too many people who feel good about promises not kept. Only make promises to your aging parents that you can keep, and then follow through.

✨ Cue Cards for Making Your Life Easier ✨

Caregivers are often so busy taking care of others that they forget there are things they can do to make their *own* lives easier. Below are some Cue Cards that will remind you how to make your role as caregiver a little more manageable.

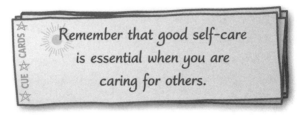

CUE CARDS ✰ ✰ ✰

Remember that good self-care is essential when you are caring for others.

You will be much more effective at taking care of others if you take good care of yourself first. Caring for your aging parents can be mentally, emotionally, physically, and spiritually challenging. Before you find yourself drained and unable to cope with what is required of you, make time to nurture yourself. Have a massage, engage in a hobby you enjoy, spend time with friends—do *something* to nurture your soul and yourself. With the time demands involved in taking care of your parents and living the other parts of your life, scheduling time for yourself may seem like an impossible task. Even if it is for ten minutes a day, make the time. If you have to schedule a short break away from the people you are caring for to make this happen, know that it is a worthwhile sacrifice for you *and* them. You will be much more effective in all of your interactions when you are in a better state of mind. Remember, it needn't cost anything to nurture yourself; the key element is devoting an uninterrupted period of time to doing something for yourself that makes you feel better.

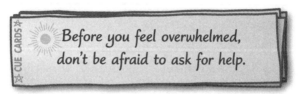

CUE CARDS
☆ CUE CARDS ☆

Before you feel overwhelmed, don't be afraid to ask for help.

If you have siblings or other family members who are able and willing to help out with the care of your aging parents, reach out to them and ask them for what you need. Many caregivers fall into the mindset that no one else can do what they do, and quite often they shoulder more responsibility than they need to. If you don't speak up and ask for help no one will know that you need it. You may be pleasantly surprised to see how many people actually come forward with assistance when they are asked.

If you do not have any relatives who are able to help, or if you live a considerable distance from your parents, many towns have programs and agencies geared to helping seniors with their needs, and in some cases the services are available for free or at a very low cost. From meal delivery to home visits, a variety of services may be offered in your parent's area. (For a quick reference list of websites for senior services, please see Resources, located at the end of the book.) Lastly, if you are the primary caregiver for your parents, you may want to consider attending a support group for people in similar situations. A support group can help you avoid the feeling of isolation that so many caregivers experience. Who knows? You may also meet someone who will be able to trade caretaking times with you so you can catch a little break here and there.

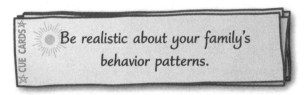

Be realistic about your family's behavior patterns.

If you have never had a close and easy relationship with your parents, it is highly unlikely that this will change once you start taking care of them. That does not mean you cannot take care of your parents; it simply means that any differences you had prior to their being in the position of needing your care are likely to persist. If you find yourself experiencing feelings of guilt, resentment, or other negative emotions related to your parents' care—emotions that keep you from implementing the suggestions offered in this book—then it may be time to seek the services of a licensed mental-health professional or support group to help you process them. Some insurance policies and Health Maintenance Organizations (HMOs) cover counseling, but if yours does not, some clinics and graduate schools offer free or very low-cost counseling. Due to the high demand for services at reduced cost, there is often a waiting list at these types of institutions; get your name on the list *before* you reach a crisis point.

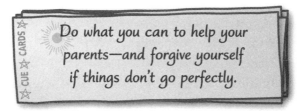

Do what you can to help your parents—and forgive yourself if things don't go perfectly.

Always remember, you can only do what you can do. Because of increasing life spans, we as individuals and as a society are sailing on uncharted waters when it comes to dealing with our aging parents. In general, seniors seem to want to hang on to their independence as long as possible while we, as adult children, may want to help our parents as much as possible. There will be times when a middle ground cannot be reached. If your parents' health and safety is in a precarious situation and your attempts to help or communicate have been unsuccessful, it may be time to get professional assistance. Sometimes aging parents are more amenable to listening to a third-party sounding board such as a family counselor, psychologist, or social worker who specializes in the care and well-being of older adults. Despite your age, education, and life experience, your parents may continue to view you as their "child" and may feel you lack the knowledge and ability to care for them. If your parents are reluctant to seek the help of a professional, remember that in their generation, mental health services were less readily available and may even have held a negative stigma. In addition, members of some cultures are uncomfortable seeking outside assistance to help resolve family issues and disagreements because they feel that sharing "private" information is not appropriate. If this describes your situation, inform your parents of the benefits of professional help but try not to get upset with them if they decline. In short, do your best to help your parents, and if your help is refused try to understand and accept the reasons why.

When you do your best to help, whether the help is accepted or not, you will find that you have fewer feelings of anger and guilt about the situation.

6 Cue Cards for the Workplace

*I*n the United States, many employers expect their employees to put in long hours, which means you need to be able to work side by side with your coworkers in a productive and amicable manner. Most people don't thrive in a hostile work environment. If a person is the cause of an unpleasant or stressful work atmosphere, at some point they will probably be fired. If a person is on the receiving end of poor treatment from a coworker, they may fail to advance in position or may even quit. As with any other relationship, miscommunication and conflict bewteen coworkers have to be addressed. The Cue Cards provided in this chapter will help make you a better employee and hopefully keep workplace conflict and miscommunication to a minimum.

It's no secret that there are many stories about workplace injustice and employers who take advantage of their employees. However, that is not the focus of this chapter. While it's true that problematic employers will always exist, if you study the Cue Cards below, they will help you become better equipped to avoid most troublesome situations at work.

✩✩ Cue Cards for Good Workplace Habits ✩✩

Let's start by looking at Cue Cards for developing beneficial workplace habits, skills you can use in just about any work environment.

CUE CARDS

Don't slack off or goof off at your job.

Learn your job responsibilities, and exercise common sense if you are asked to do something that doesn't specifically fall into your job description. You will typically have a better chance of advancement in your career if you do not adhere to a rigid "job description" approach. Be proactive and take on reasonable requests and responsibilities that you are capable of doing even if they do not fall under your job description. Also, do not pretend you are unaware of your job responsibilities:

Learn them, know them, and perform them to the best of your ability.

At the same time, learn to set appropriate boundaries at work. Going "above and beyond" what's expected may earn you a promotion, but if you are sacrificing your health or family life to work commitments, it may be time to reevaluate your job description or talk to your supervisor about your workload.

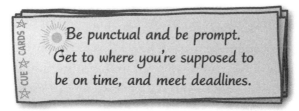

> Be punctual and be prompt. Get to where you're supposed to be on time, and meet deadlines.

If you're given a deadline, meet it. If you need to report to a meeting at a certain time, be there. Tardiness is a reflection of your ability to do your job and manage your time effectively. If you are unable to follow the simple instruction of being where you are supposed to be when asked, it is very unrealistic for you to expect your employer to believe that you will deliver on the other job responsibilities asked of you.

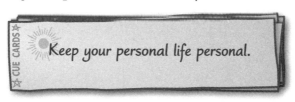

> Keep your personal life personal.

It's reasonable and normal to have a life outside of work, but don't bring your personal life to the office. In my practice, employers tell me about situations where upset spouses of employees show up or call work to try to resolve a disagreement. Obviously, this never reflects well on the employee. Also, unless your employer provides childcare, it is not appropriate to take your children to work. I once worked at a small office where we had arranged for painters to bid a job. One painter brought his wife and child with him, and we immediately eliminated him from consideration. The reason? If the family members accompanied the painter to the job site while he was working and were injured, we could potentially have been held liable. With the budget crunching that companies need to do to survive in today's environment, it is not prudent to add to a company's risk for liability. Maybe the painter would have done an excellent job, but we just could not take the chance that something might happen to his wife or young child.

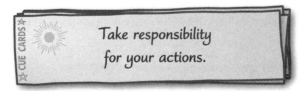

★ CUE CARDS ★

Take responsibility
for your actions.

Show that you are able to accept constructive criticism, and don't shift the blame to others as an excuse for poor performance. Believe me, most manageres are pretty astute when it comes to spotting employees who have a tendency to pass the buck. If you don't want to be passed over for a raise or promotion, take responsibility for your actions—the good and the bad.

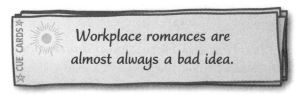

> CUE CARDS
>
> *Workplace romances are almost always a bad idea.*

We spend a lot of our waking hours in the workplace, and it is very easy to develop romantic feelings for someone you are attracted to there. As clichéd as this advice may sound, it is still, and will always be, very valid. Workplace romances are nearly always fraught with problems. What happens if your relationship ends and you still have to see and interact with each other every day? Or if your former partner becomes involved with someone else, perhaps another coworker? Are you mentally prepared to watch an ex-lover go through the giddy phases of new romance with someone else? What if the situation is reversed and the coworker has to watch you fall in love with another person? What if your relationship ends poorly, or you discover that your lover is abusive or has addictions unknown to everyone else? Do you warn the new partner? Relationships between supervisors and subordinates are even more complicated. What happens if you are romantically involved with your boss and you get a promotion? Will coworkers believe that you received it based on merit? Even if you did, you can be almost certain that no one else will feel that way.

Despite all of these considerations, matters of the heart are not always controlled by logic. If you find that you absolutely must date someone in your workplace, try to keep your relationship discreet and to avoid letting it interfere with your work. Many companies have very strict policies about romantic relationships between employees. Some companies will transfer one member of the couple to another location; others may even terminate employment over an office romance. If you've developed an attraction toward someone at the office, I urge you to educate yourself about your company's policies regarding workplace romance and proceed with caution. Overall, you may be better off exercising self-control and looking for romance elsewhere. It may take more effort, but it could be worth it.

CUE CARDS

Avoid harmful gossip.

With the mainstream media perpetually covering and glorifying gossip, it may seem like this is acceptable behavior. It is not. If you want to read or watch gossip on your own time, that's one thing, but do not gossip about others at your place of work. If you have ever been the victim of office gossip, you know how hurtful it can be—and it can also have a negative impact on your career. If you tend to be the generator of gossip, your employer may feel you have too much time on your hands or are more interested in gossip than in your job. Gossip about public figures and media personalities can be a part of normal social interaction with work colleagues, but gossip about coworkers is never a good thing.

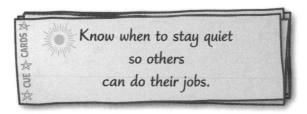

CUE CARDS

Know when to stay quiet
so others
can do their jobs.

Some individuals like to talk more than others; recent studies even suggest that some people may be hardwired to be more talkative than others. There is nothing wrong with being talkative as long as it is appropriate to the situation. If you talk so much at work that you keep others from doing their job, then you are talking too much. Supervisors and employers seldom look kindly on employees who repeatedly distract others who are trying to get their work done.

> **CUE CARDS** ☆
> Refrain from checking your personal e-mail, social media pages, and text messages while at work.

Although this tip may also seem obvious, unfortunately for some it is not. When you are at work, your employer is paying you to work for them—not to check your personal e-mail or text messages. In general, web surfing or attending to personal correspondence in any form should be avoided while you are at work as it is not what you are being paid to do. In some cases, employers view the use of office time to attend to personal matters such as phone calls, e-mail correspondence, and text messaging as "time theft" and may take disciplinary action against you for it. Perhaps it is okay with your employer if you do this during breaks or after you have "signed off" from work, but make sure you know your company's policies regarding these issues.

> ☆ **CUE CARDS** ☆
> Dress appropriately for your job.

Part of your responsibility is to represent your company favorably to the outside world, and that usually means dressing professionally. In most larger companies, dress codes are spelled out in employee manuals. If for some reason you do not have an employee manual to consult and you would like some guidelines for appropriate office wear, either ask your supervisor or note what other employees are wearing. If you are working in an office full of suits and ties, clearly jeans and tank tops will not be acceptable. When in doubt, be guided by your common sense. If you have to ask yourself, "I wonder if it's okay to wear this to work?" then it probably is not.

✫✫ Working Well with Others ✫✫

Some jobs require us to work with others. Here are Cue Cards that will help you show your supervisor that you are self-aware and know how to interact professionally with fellow employees.

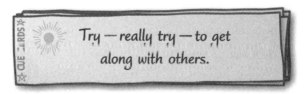

Try — really try — to get along with others.

Many individuals think the most important thing about working is to do their job to the best of their abilities. While this is mostly true, one's job performance should not come at the expense of one's interpersonal skills (aka, your people skills). Some individuals focus so much on performance that they seem to be oblivious to the fact that they are working with others. To put it bluntly, just because you do a job well does not earn you the right to be a jerk. In fact, unless you are a brain surgeon or performing some other highly skilled task, you could probably do your job a little less well if that would help you get along better with others. Though you don't need to be everyone's best friend, it is important to be kind and respectful. You will go much farther in your career if you balance likability with performance.

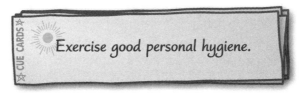

Exercise good personal hygiene.

This seems so obvious, but if it were there would be no need to mention it here. Brush your teeth, shower, use deodorant, keep fingernails well groomed and free of dirt (unless of course you work in an environment that requires you to get your hands dirty)—basically, make sure you do not have body odor or poor grooming habits that others will notice.

I once worked with someone who took garlic supplements for health reasons. He claimed they helped his immune system and protected him from colds and flu. While it is true that I don't remember his ever calling in sick, I do recall that no one wanted to sit next to him in an office meeting—he always smelled strongly of garlic. Also, if you are a fan of perfumes, cologne, or aftershave, try to go lightly on the fragrance when you are working with others. What smells great to you may not appeal to your officemates and, in some cases, may even cause an allergic reaction.

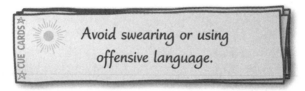

CUE CARDS

Avoid swearing or using offensive language.

Even though there seems to be an overall greater tolerance of swearing in society, it is still not appropriate for a workplace environment. You never know who may be listening and be offended by what you say, so it is always best to refrain from vulgar language while you are at work. Many people still consider swearing to be unprofessional, and when a company is paying you to do a job it is your responsibility to represent the company in a professional manner.

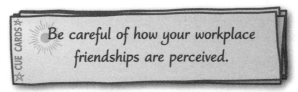

Be careful of how your workplace friendships are perceived.

It is important to pay heed to how your relationships with workplace friends are viewed. You may have formed a close but nonromantic friendship with a coworker—but will others know it is not romantic, or are you becoming fodder for workplace gossip? Some people have very vivid imaginations, so always try to keep in mind how others may perceive these friendships. To give you a specific example, years ago I worked as an executive assistant. The owner of the company didn't live far from me, and one day when his car was in the shop he asked if I would mind picking him up and taking him to work. It was on my way so I thought nothing of it. Some time later I heard rumblings that we were having an affair. I asked a few people where the rumor came from. No one would answer me until finally the office manager told me the parking lot attendant had seen us arrive together in my car one morning.

Dealing with Difficult Coworkers

Every workplace seems to have an employee or two who make it difficult for everyone else to work together harmoniously. If you have a problem with a coworker, here are some Cue Cards that should help.

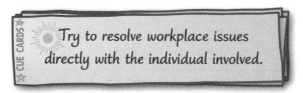

CUE CARDS ☆

Try to resolve workplace issues directly with the individual involved.

Whenever possible, dealing directly with the person with whom you're having conflict is by far your best option. Approach the coworker in question respectfully and privately, and be specific about your observations and concerns. Perhaps make a list of issues that concern you so you will be able to mention specific examples. No one likes to be told they are difficult, so a gentle approach is usually best. Strive to work toward a compromise.

Perhaps a coworker is spreading gossip about you and it is beginning to make you uncomfortable. You might say something like, "I try very hard to keep my personal life personal. Do you think you could help me with that?" Or if you are experiencing difficulty concentrating because your officemate tends to have loud telephone conversations, approach them in private and ask, "I admire how enthusiastic you are when you're on the phone, but sometimes it makes it hard for me to concentrate on my work. Do you think you could speak a little more quietly?" In both of these examples, the offending behavior is addressed privately and gently, a much more effective approach than saying, "I hear you're gossiping about me, and you really need to knock it off!" Or, "You're so loud on the phone, you drive me crazy."

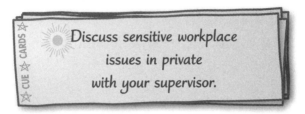

CUE ★ CARDS ★

Discuss sensitive workplace
issues in private
with your supervisor.

If you are unable to resolve a problem directly with a coworker, then it is appropriate to discuss it with your supervisor. It is part of your supervisor's job to help create and maintain a productive work atmosphere. Let your supervisor know if you have tried to resolve the issue on your own, and be specific (again, notes are helpful) about what the offending behavior is and about the steps you have taken to remedy the situation. Your supervisor may need this information in order to address the issue effectively with the employee causing the problem.

If the problem remains unresolved despite your and your supervisor's best efforts, it may be time to ask for a transfer to another area. Do not be afraid to inquire about this option;

remember, your supervisor would rather have a group of productive and happy employees than nonproductive, troublesome ones. Your supervisor's job depends on the productivity of his or her staff, so he or she will probably make the effort to improve your workplace environment when it's appropriate to do so.

✨ Cue Cards for Getting Ahead ✨

Now that you've developed good work habits and know how to work with others, let's take a look at Cue Cards that will help you advance your career and even ask for a raise.

CUE CARDS

Make a great first impression — you won't get a second chance to do so.

The saying "You never get a second chance to make a first impression" is very true. A company essentially pays you to "put your best foot forward" when representing their business—to be a goodwill ambassador for them when you are interacting with customers and associates. Be mindful of the fact that people who don't interact with you on a daily basis have no way of knowing if you are having a bad day. If they encounter you on an off day and have nothing to compare it to, they may think you are like that all the time, and that you and your company are unprofessional.

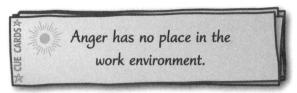

CUE CARDS

Anger has no place in the work environment.

At some point probably everyone has had a coworker or supervisor who always seemed to be angry—either about their boss or coworkers, or about their pay, working hours, or benefits, or about the work itself. The list could go on. If you are consistently angry at work, then maybe it's time for you to consider a change. No one likes a constant complainer, and your chances for advancement are slim to none if you're perceived as one. If you don't want to look for another job and find that you struggle with keeping your anger in check while at work, you may want to consider venting only to the friends you have *away* from your place of work. There's nothing wrong with venting; just keep your comments to yourself while you are "on the clock." And if you find that you are losing your non-workplace friends because you're regularly complaining, then it's time to utilize professional resources that will help you to manage your anger. It probably comes from somewhere other than workplace-related causes.

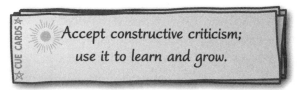

Accept constructive criticism;
use it to learn and grow.

None of us likes to make mistakes, but inevitably we will. If your supervisor comes to you to discuss a problem or offers constructive criticism, do not get defensive or blame someone else. Actively listen to what is being said and work with your boss to correct the problem. Just because your boss points out an error or wants you to make a correction does not mean that she or he is attacking your character or your worth as a person. Employers respect and value employee accountability. If your supervisor brings an error to your attention, use the opportunity to show them that you have the ability to be accountable for yourself and are able to learn from your mistakes.

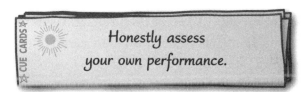

Honestly assess
your own performance.

As much as we may want more money or a higher position in a company, it does not make sense for an employer to promote or give raises to mediocre employees. The most important thing to do prior to approaching your supervisor for a promotion or raise is to give yourself an honest performance assessment. Put yourself in your supervisor's position, and ask yourself if someone like you asked *you* for a raise or promotion, would you give it? If so, why? If not, why not? If you, in your *honest* opinion, have consistently performed your job duties in an efficient and timely manner and have not been disciplined or "written up" for any issues, then a request for a raise or promotion at the time of your yearly review may be a reasonable one. On the other hand, if you regularly show up to work late or have been doing the minimum that is expected of someone in your position, then it's probably unrealistic to expect your supervisor to reward you with a raise or a promotion.

When you do approach your supervisor, keep in mind that it is okay to be confident about your work and abilities, but try to make sure your confidence does not come across as an attitude of entitlement. Do your homework and be sure what you are asking for is realistic for your position and your time with the company. It may also be helpful to research the financial health of your company before asking for a raise. Some companies flourish during economic ebbs and flows; others barely scrape by. It is unrealistic to expect a raise if your company is not doing well financially.

Closing Thoughts on Workplace Attitude...

Most employers will try their best to provide you with the skills, tools, and environment you need to do your job effectively and efficiently. If something is missing, don't be afraid to ask for it. In most cases you will find that employers are eager to hear employee feedback. When employees are happy, they are more effective and productive in their jobs—a direct benefit for any employer. Be reasonable with your expectations, address problems diplomatically when they occur, and strive to always do your best. Employers typically reward good employees, so it benefits you to be an outstanding one.

7 Cue Cards for Friendships, Parties, and Social Events

*Y*ou've probably observed that some people seem to be able to engage effortlessly with just about anyone, while others appear to fumble awkwardly through all their interactions. The reason some people handle social situations easily is because they possess good social skills.

Typically, we learn our social and conflict-resolution skills from our families; they provide our earliest exposure to a group of people we need to interact with. As children, we get a sense of what works socially and what doesn't when we relate to our family of origin. As we grow older we take the skills we learned about interacting with family members into the outside world. Usually, by the time we start applying our social skills in the real world, we have a basic understanding of how to get along with others. However, while exchanges with family members are crucial to our social development, they do not prepare us for *all* social situations.

What if a friend invites you to a party where you do not know anyone? Should you go? How do you get out of it gracefully if you don't want to attend? What about ending friendships? What happens when you have grown apart and your friend doesn't quite get the hints that you want a bit more distance? These are the types of social situations many of us will struggle with at one time or another, and they are the topic of this chapter. It's important to believe that you—or anyone— can learn good social skills. The Cue Cards that follow will help you improve yours.

☆☆ Cue Cards for Good Social Skills ☆☆

Let's start by taking a look at Cue Cards you can use in just about any type of social situation.

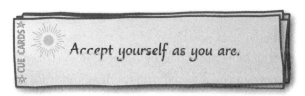

This is a big one. We tend to be our own worst critics. Some people experience a great deal of anxiety before entering into social situations because they feel that on some level they "won't measure up" to other people in the room. For quite some time I struggled with this issue myself. Prior to any type of social interaction or party, I often felt that everyone else attending was going to be a supermodel or a genius and I would be thought of as the chubby, mousy, unattractive woman in the corner. Of course, knowing that I felt this way only increased my anxiety and made me feel worse about myself—it was truly a vicious circle. One day I decided I was tired of feeling that way and wanted to do something about it. I started by simply watching how people interacted with others. I noticed that everyone who felt at ease socially was by no means a supermodel or a genius. In fact, there were often no supermodels or geniuses to be found. The people who interacted with the greatest ease were not smarter, better looking, or better dressed than anyone else; they were just comfortable in their own skin. After observing people in different social situations I would do an honest assessment of myself, and in time I realized that I wasn't so bad! Yeah, I could lose some weight or be less introverted, but really, when people interacted with me did they care about those things? No, they didn't. It seemed when I accepted myself for who I was, it was easy for me to interact with others. In short, others felt more comfortable with *me* when I felt more comfortable with *myself*.

If you struggle with feelings of anxiety when you are around others, take some time to reflect about why. Next, give yourself—or ask someone close to you to give you—an honest assessment of the perception you have of yourself and of others. Is it accurate? If so, now that you are aware of it are you able to change or improve it? In my case, my perception of others was inaccurate. Despite my imaginings, not everyone attending a party had an IQ of over 150, or was wonderfully tall, fabulously thin, and looked as though they'd walked off a magazine cover. Once I was able to pinpoint the source of my discomfort, I could objectively look at a roomful of people and realize that most of them did not possess those qualities. For me the work was changing *my* perception of others and viewing things more realistically. If your perception of yourself or others is inaccurate, like mine was, stepping back and adopting a realistic view will most likely help ease some of your anxiety and cause you to feel more comfortable with yourself.

On the other hand, if you discover that something about yourself makes you feel awkward around others, take steps to change or improve it. Don't hold yourself back from uncomfortable situations; rather, learn what makes you uncomfortable and try to improve it—always being gentle with yourself. You probably won't achieve perfection, but don't worry about it. Look around and you will see that no one else is perfect either. As mentioned, being accurately self-aware will help you feel more comfortable with yourself. In turn, others will feel more comfortable around you.

Help others feel at ease
around you.

Let others feel comfortable around you by having a pleasant facial expression and adopting open body language. Smile. If, in a group situation, you stand with your arms folded, you are sending the message that you are closed off and people should avoid you. If you are frowning, others will have a difficult time perceiving you as friendly. When you offer a smile and make yourself appear physically approachable, others will feel at ease and will approach you and engage you in conversation.

Compliment others —
but do so sincerely.

Remember that people are usually drawn to others who make them feel good about themselves. When possible, look for the positive in people, and offer sincere compliments. Looking for positive attributes is an exercise that is not limited to helping you start a conversation; it is also beneficial for your overall outlook. What I mean by this is, once you consciously start seeking good qualities in others, you may notice that your life is transformed. Don't be surprised if, after some time doing this, you start seeing the positive in other aspects of your life—your job, your love relationship, your kids. This mindset can enhance all of your relationships as well as your quality of life. Many people don't realize that they are "stuck" in negative thinking patterns, or how easy it is to fall into that mentality. With some self-training, you can fix that. I encourage you to perform the following experiment: For a day, make a commitment to find the positive in all situations and other people. See how much better you feel.

CUE CARDS

Be a gracious giver — and receiver.

Gifts should never be given with an agenda. If you give a gift, do so without conditions and expectations. Some people give gifts and on some level expect that they will get something back. Some people give gifts to get attention from others—but what happens if the attention they receive isn't to their liking? It's also important to let go of what the recipient of your gift decides to do with it. Checking to see if the person is using your gift—or is using it in the way in which you intended—is rude. Bluntly put, people should not feel held hostage by a gift they receive from you. Gift giving is about thoughtfulness and generosity; it is not about control or gaining something.

If you are lucky enough to receive a gift from someone, regardless of what it is, be thankful. Whether you like the gift or not, appreciate the fact that someone took the time to think about you. Show your appreciation by writing and mailing a handwritten thank-you note. Snail mail may be old-fashioned, but good manners are not.

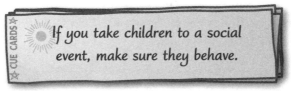

CUE CARDS

If you take children to a social event, make sure they behave.

I think all of us have been in social situations in which another person's child has "acted up" and the parents seemed oblivious to it. Your young children's behavior reflects on you, and if they are ill-behaved in public it is your responsibility to teach them how to behave appropriately. Yes, especially with young children, meltdowns happen that truly may be beyond your control, but when you are in a social setting and others are being impacted by your child's behavior, take your child outside or to a quiet room and calm them down, then come back and enjoy the party. If your partner is with you, take turns attending to your child so both of you get a chance to enjoy the event.

To avoid problems when you take your children out, it is extremely helpful to practice social skills with them at home. Teaching kids social skills helps them think beyond themselves and take others' feelings into consideration—it helps them develop empathy. Train your children how to behave in public and to say please and thank you. Take them out for social-skills practice, and role-play with them. Teach them table manners. If possible, take them out to a sit-down restaurant and teach them how to sit at a table and have a polite and quiet conversation. Show them how to use utensils, and which ones to use, and how to place a napkin on their lap. Don't be afraid to correct them when they make mistakes; this is the only way they will learn to do things the right way. Good manners and social skills will never go out of fashion and will help your children succeed in all areas of their lives. That is why it is so important for you as a parent to take the time and effort to teach them these things. Once learned, good manners are something no one can take away from your children, and they will help build their self-esteem. Teaching your children good manners and social graces is no less an investment in their future than educating them is.

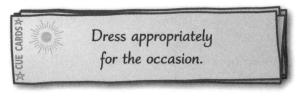

Dress appropriately
for the occasion.

When you dress appropriately for a social event, you demonstrate respect for your hosts and fellow guests and also demonstrate good social skills. Wearing something overly sexy to a family barbeque or corporate beach party will generally cause people to form impressions of you that you probably won't like. The same goes for wearing jeans to a dressy wedding. If you are unsure of what to wear, it's always a good idea to ask the host what they suggest. If this is not possible, ask others who will be attending. The added benefit of dressing appropriately for an event is that you will feel more comfortable and more inclined to enjoy yourself.

Be a good invited guest.

If you receive an invitation to a social event, whether or not you attend, you will want to keep in mind certain social "rules." If you are asked to respond to the invitation by a certain date, do so. It is perfectly acceptable to decline an invitation as long as you do so in a timely fahion and in a manner that does not hurt the host's feelings. Thank the person for inviting you and try to provide an honest reason why you are unable to attend. (If it is a situation where you would feel socially uncomfortable for some reason, it is suitable to say you have a "scheduling conflict" instead of giving the real reason for declining the invitation.)

After you have attended an event—even if it's a small dinner party at a good friend's house—consider sending the host a short, thoughtful, hand-written thank-you note via the good ol' U.S. Postal Service. While this may sound old-fashioned, it really is the most elegant and appropriate way to thank your hosts for their hospitality.

☆☆ Cue Cards for Conversations ☆☆

The ability to engage others in conversation is one of the most useful social skills you can have. Here are some Cue Cards that will help you develop this skill.

> CUE CARDS ☆
>
> Look for common ground to make conversations easier.

A good way to start a conversation with someone whom you have never met before is to look for something the two of you have in common and will be able to discuss comfortably. Is there a person in the room—perhaps the host—whom you both know? Do a quick mental check for what you and the other person might have in common. Once you find a topic, make note of it to the person, or ask a question about it.

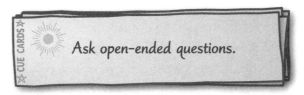

Ask open-ended questions.

Questions that have simple yes or no answers generally are less helpful in getting conversations started. As I mentioned in the chapter about communicating with your teens, the key to beginning a conversation and keeping it going is to ask open-ended questions.

For example, you're at a relative's wedding, seated next to someone you don't know. A great question to ask is, "How do you know the bride (or groom)?" Notice how this question differs from asking, "Do you know the bride (or groom)?" Phrasing the question that way can lead to a one-word yes or no answer.

If you are at a business meeting and listening to a keynote speaker, ask the person next to you what he or she thought of the speaker.

The goal with open-ended questions is to give the other person the opportunity to elaborate. This should provide you with a chance to respond, and before you know it you will have an active conversation going.

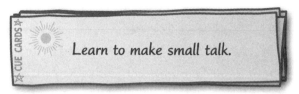

CUE CARDS

Learn to make small talk.

Small talk is the art of engaging another person in conversation while really saying very little. Individuals who are skilled at small talk are usually perceived by others as being more friendly than those who tend to keep to themselves in social situations. The thing with small talk, though, is that it must be done right to be effective. Once you begin a conversation with a new person, keep it lighthearted and limited to small talk. No matter how easy a person is to talk to, avoid making personal disclosures to someone you just met. Sex, religion, and politics are best left out of small talk because when you first meet someone it is impossible to know their point of view or how comfortable they are discussing these sorts of topics. If you share too much too soon with someone you just met, you run the risk of alienating the other person because they may be offended by something you say or see you as a person who is desperate for attention. With small talk, less is always more. If you have difficulty thinking of a subject, work on increasing your small-talk repertoire by expanding your knowledge base. Read the news, read books, watch television. Basically, stay current on community and world events, and view everything you know something about as a potential subject for small talk. Simple references to a popular television shows or news stories are usually safe bets. Try saying, "What do you think about [insert news topic or TV program here]?"

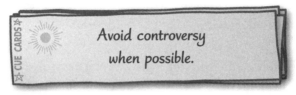

Avoid controversy when possible.

In most social situations, controversial guests tend to make other guests uncomfortable. Certain behaviors typically should be avoided at parties. Specifically, don't drink too much, don't swear, and don't flirt. No one wants to watch someone get drunk and end up spending much of the evening in the bathroom. Not only is it uncomfortable for the other guests; I have yet to meet one person who has not regretted it later when they've been the "embarrassing" guest. Likewise, swearing may be okay among your buddies or gal pals, but folks who don't know you well may be uncomfortable with it. In social situations, it's usually a good rule of thumb to watch your language. As for flirting, save this behavior for your spouse or your date. Spouses and significant others seldom welcome others flirting with their partner.

☆☆ Cue Cards for Being a Good Friend ☆☆

Now that you have all the tools you need to meet people, let's talk a little bit about what happens when acquaintances turn into friendships. Friendships are an important aspect of life. Research has shown that friendships are beneficial not only to your emotional well-being but also to your physical health. Both men and women benefit from having strong support networks. Research also indicates that what's important is not so much the *quantity* of friends one has but the *quality* of friendships. Although deeper connections are more beneficial, casual friendships are also valuable.

In general, human beings fail to thrive when they are socially isolated. If you find yourself feeling lonely and lacking friendships, you may want to take steps to remedy the situation. People who report feelings of loneliness have been found to die earlier, have reduced immunity to illnesses, and feel less capable of handling stress effectively. That being said, it is one thing to make new friends and another to keep them. Because friendships lack the formality of familial relationships, they are sometimes taken for granted, but as with any other relationship healthy friendships require work. Here are Cue Cards to help you nurture and maintain your friendships.

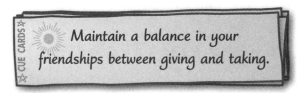

CUE CARDS

Maintain a balance in your friendships between giving and taking.

One-sided friendships are not emotionally healthy and they seldom last. If one person is doing all the giving and the other is doing all the taking, resentment will eventually set in. Friendships, like any other relationship, require balance. While you should not keep a tally sheet of the give-and-take between you and a friend, and there will be times when it is completely appropriate for one of you to give more emotionally to the other (for example, if your friend has recently experienced a loss), it's good practice to keep a general idea of what you are bringing to and taking from the relationship and aim to balance the scales accordingly.

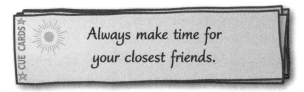

CUE CARDS

Always make time for your closest friends.

The main reason friendships end is because friends lose touch with one another. People get busy with their lives, careers, and families, of course, but it should be possible at the very least to spend ten minutes on the phone every couple of weeks just to check in with each other. If you are simply too busy to call, a quick e-mail or text to check in will let your friend know that you are thinking of them.

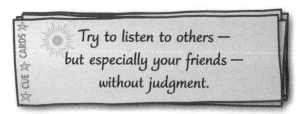

Try to listen to others —
but especially your friends —
without judgment.

There are two sides to every story, but just because your friend shares something with you it doesn't necessarily mean they want to hear your opinion. Being a source of support sometimes means simply listening without judgment as your friend vents about what's on their mind. Venting can be very therapeutic. Strive to be the safe haven your friend can confide in.

Disagree with others
respectfully.

You may not always agree with a friend's opinions or beliefs, but always strive to maintain a level of mutual respect when you disagree. Harsh words can have a long-lasting impact, so when you disagree—with anyone, for that matter—choose your words wisely.

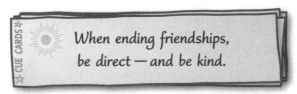

CUE CARDS

When ending friendships,
be direct — and be kind.

What happens if you and a friend gradually grow apart and no longer feel close to each other? Friendships that cause us continual stress and unhappiness are not emotionally healthy to maintain, and though it may be uncomfortable, sometimes there is no choice other than ending a friendship. When subtle hints go unnoticed or ignored, another option is to be direct about the situation. In order to minimize hurt feelings, an effective way to end a friendship is to privately tell the person you do not wish to be friends anymore. If you are asked why, be honest, but be kind. There is no reason to give a laundry list of reasons for ending a friendship, so be brief and, if at all possible, avoid placing blame, which will make an uncomfortable situation worse and exacerbate hurt feelings. You can start with something general, like, "Over time our interests and our lives seem to have taken us in different directions. I will always treasure the friendship we shared, but I think it's time for me to move on." And, yes, the "it's not you, it's me" approach is perfectly acceptable in this situation.

8 Cue Cards for Effective Apologies

*A*s mentioned previously in this book, it's usually a buildup of small thoughtless interactions that causes deep rifts between spouses, friends, and families. This is why one of the most important things you can do in your relationships is to remember that words are very powerful, so it's very important to choose them wisely. By simply taking two extra seconds to think about *how* the words you're going to say will actually be *heard*, you may easily reduce or avoid hurt feelings. Take the time and make the effort to rephrase a comment to make it less hurtful. The other option, of course, is to question whether there is any real need to make a potentially hurtful comment at all. If the comment doesn't absolutely *have* to be said, then don't say it. Believe me, you will save yourself and others much heartache if you follow this guideline.

Even if you do not intend to hurt someone and think you're being lighthearted, or helpful in a "fun" or "subtle" way, remember that "fun" and "subtle" are subjective. The person you're directing your comment to may not experience your "fun" or "subtle" words in the spirit in which you mean them. Also, if you are one of those people who likes to announce that you "just can't seem to help yourself" from "calling it like you see it," try to exercise self-control when it comes to saying something potentially hurtful. Remember, one of the differences between being an adult and a child is having impulse control—and if you control your impulse to say insensitive things, you will most likely be glad you did. When in doubt, don't say it.

Have you ever noticed that individuals who seem to have chronic communication problems are quite often victims of their own reputations? I'm referring to the type of person who seems to always manage to hurt other people's feelings or to make others angry because of something they said. In my experience, it is almost expected that this person will say something unkind or insensitive. Therefore, anything they say ends up more closely scrutinized than the comments of others who don't have frequent communication problems. Unfortunately, the poor communicator is almost always placed in a no-win situation—people *expect* them to say something thoughtless, and when they do everyone is ready to pounce on them for it. If you come away with just one useful hint from this book, let it be this: Strive not to be the person who is known as the insensitive or hurtful one. It is much easier to recover from a few misunderstandings than from a lifelong pattern of them.

As careful as you may try to be, misunderstandings and miscommunications will happen. Some people seem to think that if they let enough time go by after a miscommunication or a misunderstanding, all will be forgotten and, in essence, forgiven. While it would be nice if things worked this way, in reality they seldom do—and this is why apologies are important.

Apologies are powerful, and they also have a way of healing people both emotionally and physically. In fact, science has shown that apologies have a physical impact on the receiver. A study conducted by Hope College and Virginia Commonwealth University in 2002 revealed that heart rate, blood pressure, sweat levels, and facial tension decreased in victims of harm when they simply *imagined* receiving an apology.

Other studies have shown that a person stands a greater chance of regaining credibility and reducing the anger in a situation he or she has caused if they apologize. So apologies not only benefit the receiver; they also benefit the giver. If you ever find yourself wondering if it's worthwhile to apologize in a certain situation, the simple answer is yes.

⭐ Cue Cards for Saying "I'm Sorry" ⭐

Although there are numerous benefits to be derived from apologizing, many people find it very difficult to apologize. Perhaps even more important, it can be difficult to apologize *effectively*. If you are usually at a loss for what to say when an apology is needed, know that you are not alone. This section offers Cue Cards to get you going in the right direction.

For an apology to be considered sincere, it needs to be made up of four elements:

1. a willingness to admit you're wrong

2. an expression of regret for your actions or words (or both)

3. a request for forgiveness

4. a commitment to making and keeping your promise that it won't happen again

Let's look at these items one by one.

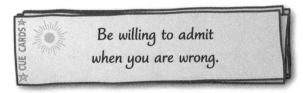

CUE CARDS

Be willing to admit when you are wrong.

When you admit you are wrong about something, you take responsibility for your actions. This is important because if you do not take responsibility for your actions and/or words, you imply to others that you have not learned from your mistakes. Basically, you are telling the other person that you feel you have permission to repeat the offense since you, in essence, "don't know any better." If it is a pattern for you to hurt others and then claim ignorance when your insensitive actions are brought to your attention, people will think you either are not very bright or are very rude, neither of which is a flattering perception. If you are wrong, simply admit it.

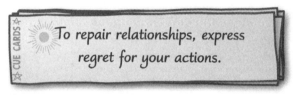

To repair relationships, express regret for your actions.

When you apologize, it is much more effective and meaning-ful if you mention the specific action you are apologizing for. A nonspecific or "catch-all" apology (e.g., "If I've done any-thing to hurt you, I apologize") is ineffective because, once again, it does not show that you have learned from your mis-take. A nonspecific apology tends to leave the receiver feeling like you're just "going through the motions" and offering lip service rather than expressing a sincere willingness to accept responsibility. For another person to believe that your apol-ogy is sincere, you must express remorse about the specific transgression.

Asking for forgiveness is a crucial element in offering a sincere apology. It is also important to remember that, even though you ask for it, forgiveness is up to the receiver to give. A request for forgiveness doesn't need to be a complicated collection of thoughts and feelings. After you've admitted you are wrong and expressed remorse, a simple "Please forgive me" or "I hope you will forgive me" is usually adequate.

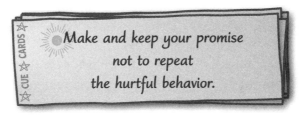

When you make a promise and keep it, it shows others you are aware and watchful of your transgressions. In relationships, as with any other area of life, you are only as good as your word. If you keep promising that your behavior will change and it doesn't, you will lose your credibility. Your promises of change and expressions of remorse will be seen as empty words.

✩✩ **Examples of Effective Apologies** ✩✩

Let's look at some examples of effective apologies. Of course, you should use these only as a guideline; tailor your apology to your specific situation.

Since we spend the majority of our time with our spouse or romantic partner, there's a pretty good chance you will need to apologize to her or him every once in a while. While most of us strive to avoid being insensitive or hurtful to our partner, we are still human and mistakes *do* happen. If you have an argument or disagreement and wish to make amends, rather than ignoring the transgression, I promise you, you have a greater chance of moving back into your partner's good graces if you offer a heartfelt apology for your part in the situation. When you apologize to your partner you send the message that they are important to you, that you care about their feelings, and that, despite what happened, you have a desire to make things right.

Let's say you've arranged to meet your partner at a certain time and you show up *very* late. Your partner is angry. The easiest way to avoid this situation would have been to show up on time, but for whatever reason that didn't happen. The worst thing you can do is to ignore your partner's feelings and pretend nothing is wrong. Using the elements of a sincere apology described above, here is what an appropriate apology may sound like:

I'm sorry I'm late. I know I should have called, but I was so wrapped up in thinking about my day that it slipped my mind. By the time I got here, I realized I was a whopping forty-five minutes late. I'm sorry I kept you waiting and I'm sorry I didn't call. It was irresponsible of me. I promise I will not let it happen again. Will you forgive me?

With this apology, the partner who was late takes responsibility for their actions, expresses remorse, promises not to repeat the behavior, and asks for forgiveness. While this may seem rather lengthy for an apology, consider the argument that could (and probably would) ensue if he or she didn't apologize. The length of the apology is necessary in order to incorporate all the elements needed to make it effective and heartfelt. And really, isn't it better to be a bit long-winded than to argue with your partner for the rest of the day?

I understand that it may seem awkward to use all four apology elements when you first try this approach, but through repeated practice it will become easier for you.

If you have time to formulate your apology before you deliver it, it is usually a good idea to rehearse it a few times to see how it sounds and make sure you're not leaving anything out. Remember, no one ever said apologies were easy—that's why I recommend you stay out of situations where you have to make them. But when you do have to apologize, doing it as described in this chapter will give you a higher probability of mending fences quickly.

The Cue Cards in this chapter will not only help you get back on track in your love relationships, they are effective for *every* situation. Let's look at an example of an apology from one coworker to another.

Your boss goes on vaction and leaves you a specific payment to mail to a vendor. When your boss returns, you realize to your horror that the payment is still in your desk drawer. Mailing it completely slipped your mind while you were handling other matters in your boss's absence. Let's say your lack of follow-through cost the company fifteen thousand dollars in late penalties. Even though you may be panicked about losing your job, it is worth your while to take responsibility for your actions and offer a sincere apology. Because you're in a situation where you know your boss will be angry and question your ability to follow directions, deflecting her anger and earning some credibility could help to save your job. An effective apology that incorporates the four elements may sound something like this:

> *I just realized the check is in my drawer and I didn't send it out. I remember your telling me how important it was that I send it while you were away, and I feel terrible that I didn't do so. I am very sorry.*

I should have taped the check to my bulletin board so I'd see it. I apologize and promise it won't happen again. I hope you will give me a chance to prove that to you.

Long-winded? Yes, but although your boss may still be angry, once she has had some time to collect her thoughts, she will probably be less angry after your apology because you will have demonstrated the ability to accept responsibility and the insight to know that what you did was wrong.

Lastly, for illustration's sake, let's look at a couple of non-apologies. I mentioned earlier how sometimes people are inclined to pretend that nothing happened, in the hope that time will heal the bad feelings about the transgression. The other thing people seem to do is skimp on one or more of the elements, which in essence results in a nonapology. If you have been the recipient of a nonapology, I'm sure you will agree that it's probably worse than no apology. Here are two examples:

"I'm sorry I was late, but you've run late before, too."
"I'm sorry if what I said offended you, but I think you're too sensitive."

The "I'm sorry, but" approach is never an effective way to smooth things over. Often, all it does is make the recipient angry—and with good reason. When apologies lack one of the four elements, they come across as insincere. When you go so far as to toss in a "but you," you send the message that even though you were wrong, the other person is also at fault. You're adding insult to injury...literally. The objective of an effective and heartfelt apology is not to share or shift blame; it is to fully accept blame and to express remorse for your behavior. If you refuse to take responsibility for your actions, then you are probably better off not apologizing. People aren't stupid, and no matter how convincing you think you're being, if you fail to take responsibility or you try to shift the blame, others will pick up on it. When this happens, not only will the issue of your transgression remain unresolved, but you will be perceived as lacking credibility. In short, your issues will snowball. Everyone makes mistakes, and learning to apologize effectively will benefit every relationship in your life—this I guarantee.

9 A Closing Note

Not all relationships are comfortable or problem free, but even those that bring us the most joy and seem to endure without much attention require work on some level. Relationships are always changing. New experiences, both good and bad, shape our personality in some way, sometimes for the better, sometimes not. It is important to keep in mind that people bring their own unique experiences into a relationship and continue to do so throughout the course of your connection with them. Your relationships with people will change over time because life changes. You, too, bring unique experiences to your relationships, and they shape the way you feel and respond to other's thoughts and feelings. I always tell my clients that our relationships, no matter how good they are, are never static—they are constantly evolving. The relationships that last seem to be between individuals who have a good working knowledge of relationship skills and are not lazy about using them.

Relationships that are worth keeping can add a great deal to your happiness and quality of life. My first hope is that in this book you have found enough guidance to hone your relationship skills and work through the majority of rough spots you'll encounter with others. My *greatest* hope is that you will be able to help others with your newfound skills.

Caregiver Checklist

☆　　☆　　☆

If you take proactive steps in caring for your parent, you may be able to prevent some age-related issues such as a slip or a fall, and avoid potential family arguments about decisions regarding health care issues. Below is an easy-to-follow checklist—or as I like to call it a "to do" list—of items that will help you in caring for your aging parent.

Discussion Points

❏ Work with your parents to create a plan of care that works for them and for you.

❏ Discuss the need for wills and living trusts.

❏ Discuss the importance of advance directives and a durable power of attorney for health care.

Keeping Them Safe at Home

❏ Determine if your parents are having problems with balance.

❏ Are there uneven flooring surfaces?

❏ Are area rugs securely in place?

❏ Are there grab bars in showers and bathtubs?

❏ Are there grab bars near toilets?

❏ Take precautions and prepare for emergencies.

❏ If you hire help, check references.

Keeping Important Information Handy

❑ Create a list of useful phone numbers for your parents: 911, ambulance, fire department, police department, relatives, neighbors, utilities, handyman, Meals on Wheels, caregiver, etc.

❑ Keep a copy of the names and contact numbers for your parents' physicians.

❑ Have your parents' insurance information on file.

❑ Keep a list of your parents' medications and supplements handy.

Checking Their Health Status

❑ Encourage your parents to get a complete physical exam.

❑ Determine if your parents are having problems with mobility.

❑ Look for signs of memory loss and cognitive decline.

❑ Check the refrigerator for oddly placed items.

❑ Are there any changes in the overall cleanliness of the home?

Making Their Lives Easier

❑ Be a patient advocate for your parents.

❑ Encourage your parents to stay physically active.

❑ Encourage your parents to be socially active.

❑ Discuss the caregiving schedule and delegation of responsibilities with siblings and other family members.

References

✯ ✯ ✯

Chapter 4

National Center on Addiction and Substance Abuse at Columbia University (CASA). *2007 National Survey of American Attitudes on Substance Abuse XII: Teens and Parents*. http://www.casacolumbia.org/absolutenm/?a=499 (accessed September 28, 2012).

Neumark-Sztainer, D., M. E. Eisenberg, J. A. Fulkerson, M. Story, and N. I. Larson. 2008. Family meals and disordered eating in adolescents. *Pediatrics and Adolescent Medicine* 162 (1): 17–22.

Chapter 8

Witvliet, C. V. O., E. L. Worthington, Jr., and N. G. Wade. 2002. Victims' heart rate and facial EMG responses to receiving an apology and restitution. *Psychophysiology* Supplement 39, S88.

McCullough, M. E., and C. V. O. Witvliet. 2001. The psychology of forgiveness. In *Handbook of positive psychology*, ed. C. R. Snyder, 446–58. New York: Oxford University Press.

Witvliet, C. V. O., T. E. Ludwig, and D. J. Bauer. 2002. Please forgive me: Transgressors' emotions and physiology during imagery of seeking forgiveness and victim responses. *Journal of Psychology and Christianity* 21: 219–33.

Resources

Therapist Search Engines

American Association of Marriage and Family Therapists
www.therapistlocator.net

American Psychological Association
http://locator.apa.org

The National Board for Certified Counselors
www.nbcc.org/counselorfind

National Social Worker Finder
www.helppro.com/NASW/Default.aspx

Gay Lesbian International Therapist Search Engine
www.glitse.com

Domestic Violence Referral Information
The National Domestic Violence Hotline
Hotline advocates are available for victims and anyone calling on
their behalf to provide crisis intervention, safety planning, information, and referrals to agencies in all fifty states, Puerto Rico,
and the U.S. Virgin Islands. Assistance is available in English and
Spanish, with access to more than 170 languages through inter-

preters. Anonymous and confidential help is available twenty-four hours a day, seven days a week.

(800) 779-7233   (800) 787-3224 (TTY)

www.thehotline.org

The National Network to End Domestic Violence

Confidential help and referrals offered twenty-four hours a day, seven days a week in up to 170 different languages through an interpreter.

www.nnedv.org/resources/stats/gethelp.html

To print a free copy of the *Domestic Violence Awareness Handbook*, please visit:

www.dm.usda.gov/shmd/aware.htm

Resources for Seniors in the United States

United States Administration on Aging

Information about resources to connect older persons, caregivers, and professionals to important federal, national, and local programs.

www.aoa.gov/elders_families/index.aspx

Administration on Aging

Information about home and community based resources for seniors in the United States.

www.aoa.gov/AoARoot/Index.aspx

Meals on Wheels Association of America

Information about meal delivery for seniors in need. To see if this

service is available in your area, please visit:
www.mowaa.org/page.aspx?pid=480

Eldercare Locator

A public service of the U.S. Administration on Aging that helps people connect to services for older adults and their families.
www.eldercare.gov

National Council on Aging

Resources and information for aging adults and their families.
www.ncoa.org

Resources for Seniors in Canada

Seniors Resource Network

Information about Canadian Government and other national organizations that offer services for seniors.
www.seniors.cimnet.ca/cim/19C44_50T1485.dhtm

Public Health Agency of Canada

This website lists resources and information available for seniors in Canada.
www.publichealth.gc.ca/seniors

United States Medical Board Websites

Alabama: www.albme.org
Alaska: www.commerce.state.ak.us/occ/pmcd.htm
Arizona: www.azmd.gov
Arkansas: www.armedicalboard.org
California: www.medbd.ca.gov

Colorado: www.dora.state.co.us/medical

Connecticut: www.ct.gov/dph/site/default.asp

Delaware: http://dpr.delaware.gov

District of Columbia: www.dchealth.dc.gov/doh/site/default.asp

Florida: www.doh.state.fl.us/mqa/Profiling/index.html

Georgia: http://medicalboard.georgia.gov/portal/site/GCMB

Hawaii: http://hawaii.gov/dcca/pvl/boards/medical

Idaho: http://bom.idaho.gov/BOMPortal/Home.aspx

Illinois: www.idfpr.com/dpr/WHO/med.asp

Indiana: www.in.gov/pla

Iowa: http://medicalboard.iowa.gov

Kansas: www.ksbha.org

Kentucky: http://kbml.ky.gov

Louisiana: www.lsbme.la.gov

Maine: www.docboard.org/me/me_home.htm

Maryland: www.mbp.state.md.us

Massachusetts: http://profiles.massmedboard.org/MA-Physician
-Profile-Find-Doctor.asp

Michigan: www.michigan.gov/mdch/0,1607,7-132-27417_27529
_27541-58914--,00.html

Minnesota: https://www.hlb.state.mn.us/BMP/DesktopModules
/ServiceForm.aspx?svid=30&mid=176

Mississippi: www.msbml.state.ms.us

Missouri: https://renew.pr.mo.gov/licensee-search.asp

Montana: http://bsd.dli.mt.gov/license/bsd_boards/med_board
/board_page.asp

Nebraska: www.hhs.state.ne.us/licensing.htm

Nevada: www.medboard.nv.gov

New Hampshire: www.nh.gov/medicine/consumers

New Jersey: www.state.nj.us/lps/ca/list1.htm

New Mexico: www.nmmb.state.nm.us

New York: www.op.nysed.gov/opsearches.htm

North Carolina: www.ncmedboard.org/consumer_resources

North Dakota: www.ndbomex.com/SearchPage.asp

Ohio: http://med.ohio.gov

Oklahoma: www.okmedicalboard.org

Oregon: www.oregon.gov/OMB

Pennsylvania: www.dos.state.pa.us/bpoa

Rhode Island: www.health.ri.gov/partners/boards/medical
licensureanddiscipline

South Carolina: www.llr.state.sc.us/pol/medical

South Dakota: www.sdbmoe.gov

Tennessee: http://health.state.tn.us/licensure/default.aspx

Texas: http://reg.tmb.state.tx.us/OnLineVerif/Phys_NoticeVerif.asp

Utah: www.dopl.utah.gov

Vermont: http://healthvermont.gov/hc/med_board/bmp.aspx

Virginia: www.dhp.virginia.gov

Washington: www.doh.wa.gov/licensing

West Virginia: www.wvbom.wv.gov/licensesearch.asp

Wisconsin: http://drl.wi.gov

Wyoming: http://wyomedboard.state.wy.us/roster.asp

Canadian Physician Information Websites

Alberta: www.cpsa.ab.ca/Homepage.aspx

British Columbia: https://www.cpsbc.ca

Manitoba: www.gov.mb.ca/health/guide/9.html

Newfoundland and Labrador: www.cpsnl.ca/default.asp?com
=Pages&id=86&m=377

Northwest Territories: www.practicenorth.ca/index.php?page
=links

Nunavut Territory: www.hc-sc.gc.ca/index-eng.php

Ontario: www.cpso.on.ca/docsearch

Quebec: www.hrsdc.gc.ca/eng/corporate/about_us/index.shtml

Yukon Territory: www.yukonmedicalcouncil.ca/physician
_licensing.html

Index

☆ ☆ ☆